COSMIC ENERGY
The Creative Power

COSMIC ENERGY

The Creative Power

Mary Ellen Flora

CDM Publications   *Everett, Washington*

Cover Art: Jeff Gibson

Art: Gail Coupal, Jeff Gibson, Mark Eaton, Holly James and
    Susan Pereira

Illustrations: Mark Eaton and Gail Coupal

Author Photo: Michelle Guilford, Yuen Lui Studio

"A Walk and Talk With God" Copyright © 1995 by Gail Coupal

Please direct requests to:

CDM Publications
2402 Summit Ave
Everett, WA 98201

First Printing 1995

Printed in the United States of America

Snohomish Publishing Co, Snohomish, WA

Library of Congress Catalog Number: 95-67294

ISBN 1-886983-00-3

Other Books Offered by CDM Publications

by Mary Ellen Flora

The Key series of books and tapes

Meditation: Key to Spiritual Awareness
Healing: Key to Spiritual Balance
Clairvoyance: Key to Spiritual Perspective
Chakras: Key to Spiritual Opening

by M.F. "Doc" Slusher

I Believe: Sermons

Acknowledgments

I wish to thank Lembi Kongas for her creativity and enthusiasm in the production of this book.

The artists who contributed are greatly appreciated. Thank you to Gail Coupal, Jeff Gibson, Mark Eaton, Holly James and Susan Pereira.

I am grateful to Diane Olson for editing and proofreading, to Diane Brewster and Deb Martin for proofreading, to Marie Senestraro for computer assistance and to the Board of Directors for financial support.

Many thanks to everyone who continues to encourage me to write. Special thanks to my loving husband M. F. "Doc" Slusher for his support and amusement.

With great appreciation, this book is dedicated to spiritual teachers both known and unknown.

CONTENTS

ILLUSTRATIONS

Introduction

Cosmic energy is an enormous subject and is impossible to cover in one small book or even in many volumes. Rather than attempting to write what I know about it, I will introduce you to cosmic energy and help you learn to discover it in your own way and time. It is more fun to get an introduction and then experiment with the subject yourself.

I have been consciously using cosmic energy to create my experience for many years. I have also taught others to do the same. It is easy and fun to use the infinite vibrations available to us to fashion our reality. We do not need to be serious about using energy. In fact, amusement can help us use energy easily without effort.

By using cosmic energy, we can free ourselves from the limits of the Earth and move to a level of spiritual awareness. We can use cosmic energy to heal, to create, to communicate and in every aspect of living and being. We can use it in meditation and in daily life.

By using different vibrations, we can create a variety of states of consciousness. We can raise and lower our vibration according to what we need or what circumstances require. We can use vibrations to be neutral, to be amused, to be earthy or to be in any state of being we choose.

Cosmic energy is the infinite variety of vibrations of the Cosmos. It can be experienced in many ways such as light, sound and color. Cosmic energy is the spiritual force with which we create matter and form our physical reality. Cosmic energy is the spiritual force of which we are made and with which we create as spirit. An understanding of cosmic energy can be gained by studying physics, but I will stay with the spiritual perspective.

The more you learn to use cosmic energy, the more you can experience your spiritual self in your physical body. Cosmic energy helps you bring the vibration of your body up to a level where you, the energetic spirit, can use your body. By manipulating cosmic energy, the spiritual being can energize its body and lower its own vibration to allow spirit and body to harmonize. When spirit can enter and create through its own body, it is able to accomplish what it wants. It is necessary to understand and use cosmic energy to do this to the fullest extent.

At this time on our planet, there is an in-flow of cosmic energy. This flow into our world is causing a great deal of change in the planet and in everyone and everything on it. We and our world are in a tremendous process of growth. We are experiencing this growth in many ways such as the natural upheavals of volcanoes, earthquakes, floods, hurricanes and other Earth changes. We are also experiencing the higher vibration in our rapidly changing social structures, as evidenced by the decline of communism and the upsurge of national independence and individuality. The social changes are seen in both destructive and creative fashion as in war and in emerging human development.

The in-flow of cosmic energy is changing everything and bringing the vibration of the planet and of our bodies up so we can have more of our spiritual selves in our physical world. This causes our bodies and all of our creations to change and spiritualize. This rapid and dynamic change brings out the best and the worst in everything. The recent earthquakes in California were a disaster, yet many people spoke of the increase in human kindness as people reached out to each other. Every experience, even the most difficult, is an opportunity to operate spiritually.

Cosmic energy flows from the Cosmic Consciousness or God. We spiritually know how to receive this energy and use it. Most people need to be reminded how to use it physically. Everyone needs to realize that there is no need to fear what is happening because everything is of a spiritual nature. This can be a time of celebration since it is the time for us to awaken into greater spiritual awareness. We need to remember that we can consciously manipulate this in-flow of energy to benefit us even if the physical world is in an upheaval.

We can best awaken to this spiritual opportunity through enthusiasm and joy. We are meant to use this power of cosmic energy to create and learn, so we can mature. Just as children are encouraged by their parents to experiment with their environment, to learn and grow, we are encouraged by our Creator to do the same. We, as spirit, are here to learn how to create, and we learn through experience. We are being given more energy to work with to accelerate our growth process on planet Earth.

My spiritual growth has been made possible by the constant and continuing use of cosmic energy. By learning to let this energy flow through my body, I have cleansed a great deal of unwanted energy and increased the desired energy flow. I use cosmic energy to clear away fear and doubt, so I can have the experience of love and enthusiasm. By clearing pain I can have joy. Cosmic energies provide a cleansing flow and a rejuvenating power.

I recently helped a young woman use cosmic energy to heal herself. She freed herself from the bonds of physical limits, within which she had been living, by using cosmic energy to cleanse past pain and regain her spiritual perspective. When she started her healing process, she believed that she hated her body. By the time she had worked for an hour with cosmic energies to clear old fears, she saw that she loved her body. It created a vast difference in her experience of life to create through love instead of through hate. Her conscious use of cosmic energy made it possible for her to create this change.

Creating with cosmic energy is a continuing process. You need to use cosmic energy just as you need to breathe. If you have a body, you have to let the cosmic energy flow through it to stay in touch with the Cosmic Consciousness and to manifest yourself. By using cosmic energy consciously, you help the whole planet and everyone on it. By cleansing your part of the world, you do your share and everyone benefits.

The Creative Power

I have recently expanded the use of cosmic energy from bringing it through my personal space to facilitating the flow of energy through a group. I did personal work and helped others with their personal focus for sixteen years before using the energy in an expanded manner. The power generated, as the group uses cosmic energy, is spectacular, and it definitely has an effect on wherever it is focused. I have done many healings cooperatively using cosmic energy. By focusing cosmic energy as a group, we have been able to help people heal very rapidly. We have also helped the in-flow of cosmic energies into the Earth to enhance the present growth process for humanity.

The power available to us is unlimited. Cosmic energy is the way this power is given to us. By learning to use this energy, we regain our place as creators on Earth. We are part of the Divine Force of God, and cosmic energy is the substance we use to manifest our Divinity on Earth.

COSMIC ENERGY

Cosmic energy is the flow of energy from the Cosmic Consciousness. It can be thought of as the creative force of the Cosmos. In modern physics, energy and matter are considered equivalent ($E=mc^2$), thus cosmic energy is the force from which all things are made. Spiritually speaking, it is sustenance from God.

Cosmic energy takes many forms in our physical world. It can be seen when it is in a dense slow form and is usually physically unseen in a fast moving form. When the energy moves slowly, we can see it as physical things. When it flows very fast, we usually cannot see it. We do not see atoms, but we do see rocks.

The electromagnetic spectrum has only a narrow range of wavelengths that make up the visible portion. Our physical eyes are blind to all but a small amount of electromagnetic energy. We can see these energies with our spiritual eye. We can learn to use these energies to create and change our reality.

There are an infinite number of cosmic energies. If we categorize them into seen and unseen energies, it helps us comprehend the magnitude and understand how we can use these energies without feeling overwhelmed. Some unseen energies are radio waves, microwaves, infrared rays, ultraviolet rays, x-rays and Gamma rays. The energies we can see manifest all around us in our world and can be seen throughout our galaxy, the Milky Way. We can see the slow moving energy manifesting in all of nature, such as in stars, trees, human bodies, plants, furniture and a long list of other physical things.

We are discovering new ways to use both the seen and the unseen energies daily.

Sometimes we are able to accept the variety of ways we can use and manipulate energies, but we often get a mind set about how to use the full range of energies available to us. For example, we now believe that we can use microwaves to cook food but may not believe we can use other cosmic energies to heal the physical body. We believe that we can see pictures on television sent from unseen waves of energy. Yet, most people are skeptical about visualizing mental image pictures and auras.

As spirit, we have the knowledge and ability to use cosmic energy consciously. We can manipulate cosmic energy to create. We can use it to change or heal, as with laser energy, and we can use it to communicate as with radio waves. We have, unfortunately, forgotten most of what we know about cosmic energy. Only a fraction of our great knowledge is still being used.

Cosmic energy is what all things are made of and by which all things are maintained. It is the energy from God with which God created all things and sustains all things. Religion and science come closer together every year as new discoveries come to light. It is only in recent history that humans remembered that energy and matter are equivalent, thanks to Albert Einstein. We were lost in the density of matter and forgot its origin in energy.

Everything is energy. God is energy. God is the center and source of all energy. Spirit is energy. When we realize that everything is energy, we are freed from the limits of the world of matter. Whether we are viewing our hand or the universe, we can see that energy can be manipulated to create change.

We are spirit. We are a very high vibration of energy. We have created physical bodies to create through, and these bodies are a low vibration of energy. We and our bodies are created from cosmic energy or God's energy. We can physically see bodies because they are a low vibration. The energy in bodies moves slowly enough for the physical eye to perceive it. Spirit is seldom seen by the physical eye since its energy moves so rapidly. Spirit is such a high vibration, it is usually seen only with the spiritual eye.

As spirit, we are learning to use cosmic energy to create just as God creates with this energy. We use our bodies to focus our energy and as a vehicle through which to create. We have to learn to slow our high spiritual vibration to relate to a body. We also have to learn to increase the energy in the body to allow ourselves as spirit to move more into the body. Learning to work with a body is a major lesson for all souls. It is part of the lesson about how to manipulate cosmic energy.

Planet Earth is a school for souls needing to learn how to manipulate energy. We are here creating, destroying and learning. Like all children, we make mistakes, forget our lessons, ignore our Parent and rebel. Unfortunately, we have been so juvenile we have even forgotten our origin. We have rebelled to the point of forgetting we come from God and are meant to return to God. We are energy and will return to our Source of energy. We have forgotten everything is energy and a part of God. God is energy. God is everything.

When we remember who we are and what we are here for, we will rapidly mature into the enlightened beings we are meant to be. First, we have to remember that we are spirit, a part of God, and everything is energy. We also need to remember that we can manipulate energy to create our reality and heal ourselves and our world. These realizations give us a new perspective of the world and our place in it. We are here creating the world with seen and unseen energies. We make the world beautiful or ugly according to how we use energy.

Vibrations are the simplest way to relate to cosmic energy. Vibrations can be translated into colors which we can then easily relate to physical reality such as emotions or other states of being. Cosmic energy can also be seen as formulas and equations, but most people do not relate well to this form of communication. Music is a form of vibration most of us relate to well. We can feel the vibration of music and relate it to our emotions and other body communications. Color is still the simplest way to translate vibrations into physically comprehensible terms.

There are an infinite variety of vibrations. These can be translated into every conceivable color. These vibrations can be used to form our reality. The vibrations can be clear and light or dark and dense depending on the motion of the vibration. The faster the vibration, the clearer and lighter the color. The slower the vibration, the darker and more dense the color. White is a high vibration and orange is a lower vibration.

If you add white to the orange, it increases the vibration and makes it lighter. If you add more orange, it becomes a lower vibration. Basic art and music lessons teach us a great deal about energy.

Unless you want to study art, music, physics or some other discipline focused on energy, the best way to learn about cosmic energy and use it is to meditate. Through meditation, you can tune into a tremendous variety of vibrations and learn how they affect you and how you want to use them.

In meditation, you sit quietly and tune into the spiritual realm and yourself as spirit. In this way, you can experience various vibrations. You can experience the vibration of your body and of you as spirit. You can learn about the vibrations of Earth and of the Cosmos. By dividing energies into seen and unseen, you bring your focus to earth and cosmic energies, or to energy moving slow and energy moving fast.

The simpler things are, the closer they are to the Source or God. The more complex they are, the farther from God, the Source, and the more involved in matter. Just as the Source is one and the resultant creations are many, we progress from simple to complex. When you begin seeing spirit and body as different, you discover that spirit is simple and body is complex. If you are experiencing complexities, you are dealing with your body. If you find things to be simple, you are operating as spirit.

Through meditation, you can learn how to focus on the simple and release the complex. You can learn how to manipulate energy to simplify your reality. When you do this, you move out of the slow vibration of the body into the faster vibration of spirit. You move from the many of the physical to the One of spirit.

Cosmic energy has been translated into vibrations, colors and meanings by many beings. While these interpretations can be helpful, it is recommended that you learn to translate these for yourself. Colors have a variety of meanings and need to be interpreted according to the present circumstances. If you follow someone else's ideas completely, you will not learn your own interpretations.

You can use generalizations about colors without becoming dogmatic about the meanings to give you some structure without limiting your freedom. The lighter and brighter a color, the higher or faster the vibration. The darker and denser the color, the lower or slower the vibration. There is no good or bad about fast or slow, high or low. All vibrations are necessary for things to be as they are. Just as the electricity in a light bulb needs positive and negative energy to produce light, we need different energies to manifest our creations.

Other generalizations about colors include common translations into states of being. A few of these are: light red - life force energy, dark red - anger or disturbance; light green - growth and healing, dark green - past time; clear dark blue - certainty, dense dark blue - responsibility for others; light yellow - vitality, dense yellow - intellect. This list can go on forever. It is easy to see why it is important to learn to interpret colors for yourself. You could spend a lifetime memorizing someone else's list of translations and still not have the correct one for a particular circumstance.

It is much easier to learn to meditate and interpret your own spiritual information.

Each vibration has a different effect. Each soul has a different response to each vibration. You discover the effect of and your response to vibrations by meditating. Because you are energy, you affect every other energy. When you meditate, you learn how you are vibrating and how you affect things around you as well as how things affect you.

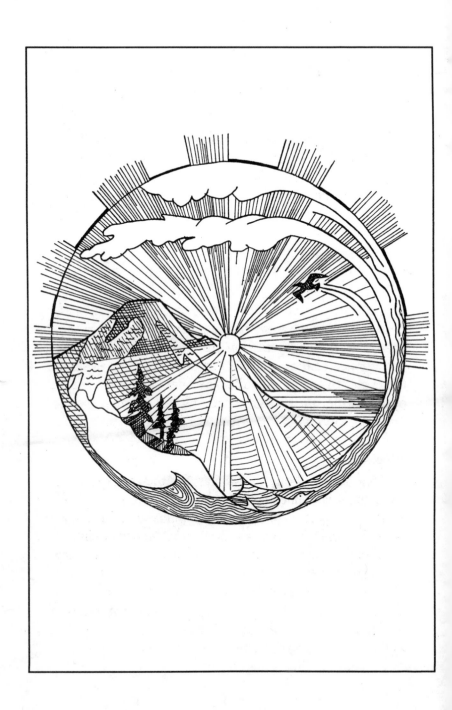

ALL ENERGY IS CONNECTED

Our solar system is an example of the connectedness of all things. We have learned to observe the effect of the planets on each other and the effect of the sun and moon on the Earth. The science of astronomy is devoted to the study of the heavenly bodies from an intellectual perspective. The scientific information supports a great deal of the spiritual perspective. One important area of agreement is that everything affects everything else.

The solar system is one small part of the Cosmos that mirrors the whole system. The sun, moon and planets have patterns of interaction that maintain their balance and connectedness just like the Cosmos. For example, the cycles of the moon affect the tides on Earth, and the cycles of the sun affect the seasons. All of the planets in our solar system have an effect on Earth, and our planet also affects the entire system. Our solar system, in turn, affects everything around it.

The human body is similar to the solar system. Everything is connected. Every part of the body affects every other part. We can easily see this with our human body because we have an intellectual understanding of cells and molecules that connect all parts of the body. We can extrapolate this understanding to the solar system when we see that energy connects the planets, moon and sun just as it connects the individual parts of the human body. We can look at the larger picture and see that the Cosmos is connected by energy in the same way. Thus, all things are connected.

From the microcosm to the macrocosm, the pattern is the same. Everything is connected and interactive. This is true in both the physical and the spiritual sense. Since everything is energy, everything is energetically connected. A simplistic view is that our body is connected to the planet, Earth to the solar system, the solar system to the Cosmos. We, as spirit, are connected to our higher awareness, and that, in turn, to a higher level, and to the Cosmic Consciousness or God.

The planets of our solar system are more important to us than we validate. They represent aspects of our physical and spiritual experience. Astrologers, as long ago as the three wise men in the Jesus story, tell of the impact of heavenly bodies on the Earth experience. Astrology gives us information about how the planets affect us in our spiritual journey, what our strengths and weaknesses are, and how to best use our energies through time and space.

The planets represent and embody levels of learning you must pass through as spirit, as well as aspects you have available within yourself. They influence your behavior and encourage your growth. They manifest within you. You can reach a level of development where you can recognize them within. Close your eyes and be still, and you may see the solar system in your head. You may even see a view of the Cosmos. Meditation can bring you to this level of spiritual awareness.

The heavenly bodies provide us with a wealth of information, if we can receive it. The sun as the projecting male and the moon as the receptive female can teach us about the male and female aspects within each of us. Mars as the male and Venus as the female can also help us to understand and best use these two energies we all have. As we learn the characteristics of the planets, we learn about ourselves. Each planet has meaning for our spiritual growth since it has unique energy that can teach and influence us. Each planet represents an aspect of our spiritual self.

What happens within us affects all around us, and what occurs outside us affects us within. The energetic nature of all things connects us to everything, thus we affect everything and are, in turn, affected by everything. The magnitude of this realization can be overwhelming. A spiritual perspective is necessary to grasp this concept of Wholeness without getting overwhelmed by the intellect.

It is not necessary for you to study astronomy or astrology to take charge of your effect on the cosmos. You can turn within and be still to discover yourself as spirit. You can then strengthen yourself to accomplish your goals and take charge of your personal impact. Regardless of how much you study, you must eventually return to your inner focus to know yourself and your relationship with all other things.

To know the Cosmos, you must first know yourself. By knowing yourself, you know how you affect things, what your part is in the play, and how to best fulfill your present role. You will not learn these things by looking at the stars in the sky although they may inspire you. You will learn about the energy of all things by knowing your energy. What you do within you, you do to everything around you. Everything outside of you affects you according to the manner in which you relate to it. You are a microcosm of the Cosmos, made to learn about creation. You can learn to be a compassionate, loving creator, a cruel, hateful one, an indifferent creator or whatever you choose. Do remember that what you create affects you as well as everything around you.

You learn your impact on reality by observing yourself. You can discover the personal view of your spiritual creativity by looking at your interaction with others. You are connected to both the people you like and the people you do not like. Your relationship with these two groups will tell you a great deal about your microcosm. Learning to be accepting and loving with everyone is part of your maturation process. You can learn to love everything and everyone, even the things you do not like.

Being connected does not mean being merged. Healthy cells exist in a body without merging. Unhealthy cells merge and loose their unique purpose. There are many examples of being connected without being merged: grapes on a vine, drops of water in a river, molecules in a rock, trees in a forest. These examples tell us how to operate as separate yet connected consciousness. We are connected and separate. We are free to affect the world in our own unique fashion.

You can create the greatest benefit in your creative process by awakening to your uniqueness. As an awakened spirit, acknowledging your personal energy and impact, you can communicate and create on a conscious level. You become aware of yourself as part of the Cosmic Consciousness and create according to the Cosmic Plan. You are connected to all things. When you create with the awareness of your connectedness, life takes on new meaning. You are meant to awaken like Jesus, Buddha and the other teachers to play your part in the dance of life.

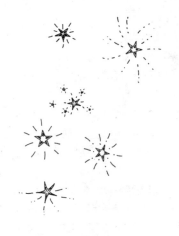

ENERGY OF THE TEACHERS AND MESSENGERS

There have been many teachers and messengers sent to us throughout the existence of humankind. These beings come to tell us the wonderful news that we are spirit and a part of God. Teachers have told their story to reach the group into which they manifested. Messengers such as the Archangels Gabriel and Michael come to tell of important events and herald spiritual changes throughout history.

Every teacher has a unique vibration. Each of the world teachers brings us a different perspective of the same story via his or her personal energy. There have been many more teachers throughout history than we have in written record. Many of the teachers who came to remind us that we are spirit and a part of God were known only to a few people. They were unknown except for their energetic impact on our reality. There are also those brave souls who volunteered as public teachers to be an example to the world.

Some of the well known teachers are Lao Tsu, Confucius, Buddha, Abraham, Moses, Jesus, Mary, Mohammed, as well as many others. Each of these souls has a unique vibration to use to teach us and communicate with us. All of these teachers are available to communicate with by any sincere seeker regardless of the spiritual path the seeker travels.

The teacher you choose to follow depends on your preference of vibration. There is a different vibration for every body type, and this may determine your attraction to a teacher. You may be the same body type in which the teacher manifested. Your choice could come from your preference of the vibration of the particular way that teacher taught. For instance, Moses vibrated on a level of law, and Jesus vibrated on a level of love. Both of these vibrations are necessary, but different souls are attracted to different paths.

A simple way to understand the significance of the different teachers is to think of them as leaders on a particular path. They are a bright light or vibration leading along a path to God. There are many paths to God. Each of the teachers leads the way on the path he or she came to show. It is up to the individual soul to decide which path to follow. Some follow the path of a well-known teacher, and some follow the path of an unknown teacher. There are also those who follow their own path.

The benefit of following a teacher is that you have the bright light ahead of you showing you the way. You have direction and inspiration. You have the reassurance that this path leads to God as the teacher has already reached that destination. You will also find fellow travelers on the main paths. A spiritual community provides support and encouragement. In some cases, there is also the written record of these teachers to guide and instruct you.

Those who choose to follow their own path can reach their destination through personal commitment. They may feel alone in their journey, at times, as they are forging through new territory. They can be an inspiration to others and may be surprised to find others following them if they look back. Every soul can be a bright light to inspire others just as the well known teachers are a light to us. Everyone is energy and can shine.

A soul must eventually choose one path, whether it is a main road of one of the world teachers or a personal trail. By choosing a path and following it, one makes a commitment. This commitment allows the soul to focus his or her attention on the path and goal. When committed or focused, all manner of events happen to make the journey possible. The soul is able to arrive at the destination with less struggle and fewer detours when focused on the journey. Focused energy is more powerful than diffused energy.

If you do not commit to a spiritual path, you find yourself unfocused and eventually unsatisfied. Being unfocused is like traveling across parallel roads instead of taking a road straight to your destination, or going in circles instead of in a straight line. Some need to sample different spiritual paths because of their doubt or fear. Others take time to discover their true path because of pain, temptations, programming or other detours. When you do find a path on which you feel at home, trust yourself and make a commitment to your path. When you stay on your chosen path, you arrive at your destination.

No path is better than another. No spiritual teacher is superior to another. A true teacher and a straight path will lead you to God. You will know a false teacher or a wrong turn by using your own spiritual abilities. If you are uncertain about your clairvoyance and knowingness, then depend on your feelings. You know how you feel. If a teacher or path feels right to you, when you meditate on it, trust yourself. If there is any doubt, turn to guidance from God. Turn within to God and you will discover your path.

The teacher with whom I am most familiar and the one I have chosen to follow is Jesus. I will also tell you a little of Mary, Jesus' mother, who is a great teacher as well. Both of these wonderful beings are available to everyone whether one is following the path on which they lead or another path.

There is a great deal of information available about the historical Jesus, so I will relate to the spiritual or energetic impact of Jesus instead. While people can argue over the historical details, it is obvious that a man would not have the worldwide influence achieved by Jesus without the intervention of God. One cannot intellectually explain his effect on the world, so we must turn to spiritual understanding.

Jesus is an evolved being who agreed to return to Earth to play the role we know of as Jesus as well as to play a much larger role as a world teacher and a force of light. He is often referred to as an archangel. Jesus was born into a body. He was trained as a man, in his society, as well as by teachers of God. He and the group around him knew his purpose and worked together toward the accomplishment of his goals. Jesus manifested the Christ and then gave his energy to change the vibration on Earth.

Jesus and the Christ are not the same. The Christ is the force of energy from God that manifested in Jesus. This Christforce manifested in all of the great teachers. Jesus told us that it can come into each of us if we prepare ourselves as he did. The Christforce is a particular vibration of God meant to manifest in humanity.

The Christforce manifested fully in Jesus when he was baptized by John. After this transformation, it was necessary for him to go through a rigorous time of testing or temptation. This confirmed that Jesus could deal with the power of the Christ without falling prey to the temptations of the physical world. Jesus proved that he could manipulate the power of the energy that he was given.

The Christforce gave Jesus power beyond our comprehension. This power was to be used to heal, teach and preach the message of God. It was not meant to benefit the physical powers which were in competition with God. Jesus had agreed with God to manifest God in the form of matter as a human. Even after his thirty years of preparation, Jesus had to pass the test and prove that he could deal with the power he had agreed to manifest. As we know, Jesus was able to create with the Christforce and spread the energy of God around and through the Earth.

Jesus created wonderful things as he manifested God's energy on Earth. He taught many more people than is recorded, and these people also brought the vibration of God into the Earth. He taught people around the world. He appeared to many of these people in his physical body. He also appeared to people in his astral body. He was able to manifest this spiritual or astral body as clearly as his physical body. He was able to appear and create in either his physical or spiritual body. He could manipulate cosmic energy to manifest whatever he needed in the physical world.

Jesus was an accomplished healer, clairvoyant, telepath and transmedium. He was adept at using his astral body, crystal body and all of the other spiritual bodies. Jesus was a spiritual adept or master. His mastery of all of his spiritual and physical abilities was necessary for him to accomplish his purpose.

His purpose was to bring the energy of God into the Earth. He did this by bringing God into himself, into his body and then into the Earth. Jesus mastered all things spiritual and physical and gave it all back to God. Jesus mastered immense power and used it to bring the energy of God into the planet. He could have used this power to create a physical kingdom, but he was strong enough to use it to bring in the awareness of the spiritual kingdom. This energy is in the Earth for all of us to use in our Christ awakening.

The message of Jesus was simple and easy to understand. He taught us to love God above all things and to love each other as ourselves. He taught in a manner everyone could understand. He gave us examples we can understand two thousand years after he was in a body. He was manifesting spirit fully, and thus was able to relate in the simplicity of spirit.

Jesus wanted everyone to see they could do what he was doing. He desired all souls to focus on God and bring forth the spirit of God within our lives. He believed in us and our ability to be all that we can be. He had so much faith in us that he devoted his entire being to the project of teaching us. He poured his personal energy and the Christforce energy he had received into the Earth and into each of us.

We have a gift from Jesus that very few beings realize. We have his energy in our vibratory system to use in our own spiritual growth. He has devoted his energy to us to help us grow and mature to the level he accomplished. He has given us himself and all he accomplished. We can do what he has done.

Mary, the mother of Jesus, is another spirit who has devoted her energy to the awakening of planet Earth. Mary has been stereotyped as "mother" to the point that most people do not see her as a teacher, healer and spiritual master. Mary is an evolved being who prepared to be the mother of Jesus. She was born into a female body and trained to play the part of the mother to Jesus. She was also his teacher as all mothers are the most important teacher of their child.

Mary was both a teacher and a student to Jesus. While Jesus was a boy, Mary was the teacher. Once Jesus grew into manhood, he became her teacher. Mary was one of his most important students. She became adept in all of the spiritual arts. She developed her clairvoyance, healing and other spiritual skills. She worked in her physical body and her astral body.

Mary traveled widely throughout the world. She taught, healed and brought the light of God to every place she visited. She learned to balance her male and female energies to the point of manifesting the Christ within herself as Jesus did.

Mary is often seen as representing the female principle of life. Mary is an evolved being with a positive-negative energy balance and not limited to the female vibration. Her representation of the female aspect is a chosen and important role but does not limit her in expressing spiritual balance. Planet Earth is now balancing its positive, negative poles to allow the Christforce to manifest fully in the planet, and Mary is an inspiration to help everyone acknowledge the female vibration.

The Earth has been imbalanced toward the male or positive vibration for a very long time. Mary is an important resource for us to relearn how to have and use the female or negative vibration. Both men and women need to learn how to use this female aspect of self and how to balance the male and female vibrations inherent in each of us. A light bulb has both positive and negative poles to generate light. This is true of us as spirit as well. We must balance our positive-negative polarity to manifest the light of spirit in our bodies.

Mary brings a female message of love, forgiveness and non-resistance. We all have a female aspect that we need to remember and use in our daily lives as well as in our spiritual development. Our female aspect helps us receive cosmic energy and the energy from God. Mary teaches us how to develop and use the female aspect within ourselves.

Love is the vibration of God we experience in a body. Love can be experienced through the entire spiritual system but is easily experienced through the fourth chakra which has a female nature. It allows us to experience the oneness with all things and the affinity that comes from that. Our female energy, as exemplified by Mary, helps us manifest love in our lives regardless of the gender of our bodies.

Forgiveness is letting go which is also a female aspect of our energy. From a spiritual perspective, forgiveness is being able to release everything of the physical world to move freely toward the spiritual realm. The vibration of forgiveness is similar to the energy of amusement, thus forgiveness is not serious but joyful in its nature.

Non-resistance is a female vibration. It is the ability to allow things to pass by or through, like the reed in the river letting the water flow by, the wheat in the field bending before the wind, or the glass allowing the sun to shine through. Non-resistance is one of the lessons Mary teaches so well. We all need to develop this quality to manifest our unique vibration instead of the other energies around us.

Mary is not like the image often portrayed of her as the sweet, mild-mannered child bride. Mary is loving, kind and gentle, and she is also strong, certain and straightforward. Mary also became a Christ and needed the strength and power to do so. She is a living embodiment of the balance of male and female energies within a soul. Mary is with us to help each of us do what she has accomplished; which is to manifest God within.

You can communicate with any of the teachers through meditation. When talking with Mary, you will find a compassionate, strong and forthright being. Her advice often includes not resisting, forgiving and loving. She also tells you clearly what her perspective is about a situation. Mary teaches us of love and life.

Angels are another group of messengers we have with us. The Archangels Gabriel and Michael are well known. There are a multitude of unknown angels to help us. They bring us a message of love, encouragement and hope. They can help us regain our spiritual perspective and communication. Angels are willing to help in our creative process. They are best known for intervening in emergencies and death experiences, but they are available to help us in everyday affairs also. Unfortunately, most people reach out to them only when they are desperate.

We need to remember that angels are always with us and can help draw our attention to our spiritual nature and reality. We have to ask for their intervention, help or communication; otherwise, they remain silent observers. By talking with them, we open ourselves to the spiritual realm and increase our spiritual awareness. Their perspective can open a new way of viewing and relating to life. Conscious communication with angels creates a new way of living.

The angels can help us with every decision in our life. There is no issue too small for their attention. Enjoy asking advice on what to wear or what to eat, to get accustomed to talking with them. If we are in the habit of talking with angels, we will find it easy to ask for help when we need it. Angels can also help create a safe environment for meditation. We tune into God when we talk with God's messengers.

God has sent us so much to draw our attention to the Cosmic Consciousness. By tuning into the vibration of the angels and other messengers of God, we remember that we are a part of this Oneness. As part of God, we remember who we are and realize our ability to create on a spiritual level.

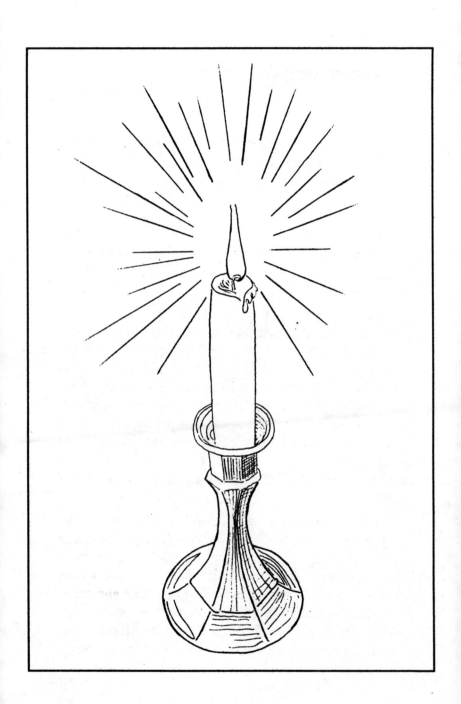

CHRISTFORCE ENERGY

The Christ is the higher self of all of humankind. We are all one when not divided by matter. The Christ is God made manifest in man. Christ is the invisible God made visible in matter. Everyone is meant to manifest God within or the Christ. Christ or the higher spiritual nature of all humankind is available to every soul. We simply need to recognize the spiritual nature of God and our own spiritual nature to see ourselves as part of the Cosmic Whole or God.

Christ translated from Greek means appointed or anointed. The anointed one is one who truly chooses God. God loves everyone. Not everyone loves God. When one loves God above all else, the Christ is able to develop fully in that soul and manifest God within. This manifestation may be for seconds, years or a lifetime. Jesus was not the only soul to manifest the Christ within. Many other souls have achieved this level of spiritual development. In fact, every soul is meant to develop to the level of manifesting God within or the Christ.

Christ is often used to indicate "God Within". The Christ is the spiritual vibration through which God can manifest through a soul creating in a body. Humanity is spirit in matter. Since matter involves time and space, the vibration of God must move through time and space to manifest in man. There is a spiritual system through which spiritual vibrations move. The Christforce is the spiritual vibration that translates God into human souls.

Christ is the energy through which God comes to us on Earth. Through the Christforce energy or Christ Ray, God communicates to us. Just as the sun brings life and light to Earth, God shines through the Christ vibration bringing spiritual light and life. God moves through all things. God moves most freely into Earth through the Christforce.

The Earth is a creation established for learning, growth and the manifestation of conscious spirit in matter. The spirit devoted to shepherd the Earth is the Christ and the Christ vibration. Many have manifested this Christ vibration in their bodies. Jesus, Buddha, Lao Tsu, Mary and all of the great teachers manifested the Christ into physical form. Through the Christ, God is able to come into physical matter and manifest for all to see and experience.

Christ is not limited to Christianity. Christ is the driving force of energy in all religions. It may be called by other names, but it is the spiritual Sun of Earth which shines into all. We need to recognize it within ourselves for it to manifest. All religions are inspired by the same Force since everything comes from the same God or Source. God uses this vibration to manifest on Earth, thus the Christforce vibration can be found in everyone. The variety and uniqueness is created by the souls and their bodies through which the Christforce flows.

Each religion had a unique inspiration and vibration at its creation. Each great teacher followed his or her own path of cleansing and devotion to prepare for the awakening of the Christ in the body. Just as each of us is unique according to what each needs to learn and teach, each religion is unique because of what it needed to teach. All of the world religions also have many similarities. The concept of a trinity is common and not unique to Christianity. The trinity is a way of expressing the translation of God to the human species, or spirit into matter. The trinity is God's vibration awakening in man through the various levels of spiritual manifestation. It expresses the part of God in man, the part connecting God and man, and God. The Christforce is the vibration through which we can most fully manifest God within ourselves. The Christforce is a ray or vibration just as the trinity is a ladder or way. The Christforce is an aspect of the trinity.

Teachers such as Jesus and Buddha are beings who were willing and able to manifest the Christ into their bodies. Over the centuries, different teachers have been sent according to the needs of people at that point in time. Each teacher has vibrated at the level of energy that could best reach the existing population. Each teacher presented the Christ Ray in the way most souls could relate to it and in the manner then needed to increase the Earth's energy.

Each religion has offered what humanity has needed to learn at a particular time in its development. Each religion builds on the one before it. Humanity awakens as it moves from Earth focus to God focus; from many gods to one God. As humanity matures, it begins to accept the magnitude of God instead of attempting to humanize God. Eventually, humanity will begin to spiritualize itself instead of trying to humanize God.

While the spiritual awareness of humankind has been kept alive by spiritual forces, the human bodies also have been developing and been helped to develop. This improvement of our bodies is necessary to create vessels to best contain the Christ we are all meant to manifest. Unfortunately, many souls have gotten lost in these capable bodies. The challenge is to use the vessel without becoming lost in it.

Even the religious bodies, developed after each great teacher, got engulfed in the patterns of matter. The religions all developed the complexity of body and lost much of the simplicity of spirit. The great religions all buried the core message of God under a mountain of dogma and rules. Religions were used to gain and wield Earthly power, and the original messages were put aside for worldly gain. Only a remnant of the message survived as the physical organization of the religions overcame the spiritual message.

Eventually a new messenger would come to Earth, and a new religion would arise to awaken humanity and carry it forward in its spiritual development. Each step provided what was needed at the time. Each religion was correct for its time and can continue to be used if the original message is followed. We need to be cautious about accepting the accumulation of worldly concepts associated with the religions and remain true to the message from God.

We as spirit reincarnate in new bodies to continue our growth and development. The message of God also reincarnates in the bodies of teachers and the corresponding religion to keep God alive in developing humanity. The Christ Ray is the vibration through which we are awakened and anointed as children of God.

Every soul on planet Earth is meant to manifest the Christ vibration and become a Christ. When we are able to experience God Within, to that extent we are ready to return to our Source. Buddha and some of the other great teachers choose to remain with us until every soul achieves this glory. Jesus gave all that he gained to us, so that we would have his energy to help us do what he did. Many souls have attained the Christ level. We also can experience God Within.

The confusion about the Christ and Christforce energy comes mostly from trying to understand the process of spiritual communication in limited terms. The new insights in science help us see the spiritual flow. We see that there was one Source from which came two, which then divided into many. The two may be called spirit and matter or positive and negative. The power caused by the divisions created the Cosmos. From this creativity, all spirit and matter were created. Our small part of the Cosmos called Earth is an expression of spirit into matter. Earth, and the creative game here, is a culmination of the creative process allowing every soul to manifest the Christforce.

We have everything in and on Earth to exemplify the experience of the Cosmos. We have dichotomies to help us learn to balance. This joining of spirit and matter called Earth is our opportunity to learn about creativity. We need to learn our spiritual level of creativity to be able to withdraw our energy from matter and return to our Source as pure energy.

Recognizing the Christ or God Within is part of our lesson. When we learn that we are children of God and that God is within us, we rise above the limits of the physical world and become part of the spiritual experience. There has always been help for the Earth, both spiritually and physically. God's many creations have always offered an abundance of assistance. Some of the names we have put on these sources are angels, archangels, cherubim and seraphim. Our helpers also include beings who have manifested in human bodies such as the teachers and beings from other planets. All of these sources of help have been raising the consciousness of humans to a level of spiritual awareness so we can recognize that God is within us.

As we awaken, we begin to see the help that is available to us and how we can use this assistance. If the intellect interferes with doubt about the validity of this help, we can realize that we believed that the world was flat not very long ago. Humanity is a sleeping giant slowly awakening. We are a soul that is an aspect of God and are just waking up to this. Christ is God Within, and we are all a Christ. In recognizing this, we awaken to our spiritual nature and our place in the Cosmic Consciousness.

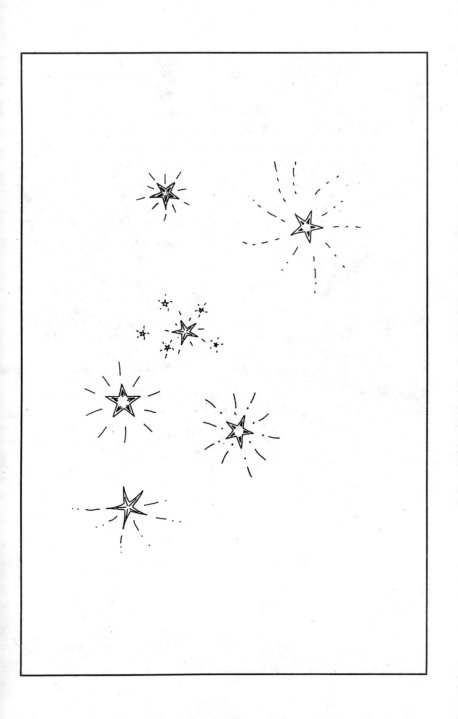

GODFORCE ENERGY

All energy originates from God. The Creator of all things is the Source of everything. Everything we know of on Earth and throughout the Cosmos is made up of the energy of God. Science is beginning to support what they call the Big Bang Theory or the idea that everything started at once from one source. Spiritually aware souls have always known this. God is one and all else flows from the One. Science and theology are moving closer together as the human species matures and becomes more intellectually sophisticated and more spiritually aware.

It is impossible to speak of all things, even from the scientist's point of view of quarks and neutrons. This discussion of God's energy will pertain to the way we on Earth relate to it and how we use it. God's energy has been referred to as manna from Heaven, which is an adequate description. It is the flow of energy from which all things on Earth are created. It is the energy which created everything, sustains all things and of which all things are a part.

Because we limit ourselves by our physical bodies and their comprehension, we must speak of God in language that the body as well as the spirit can understand. The most common mistake in gaining an understanding of God is attempting to humanize our Source. We must keep in mind that we cannot fully comprehend the magnitude of God while in a body. We need to do our best to live what we know of God instead of intellectualizing God.

41

Both the spiritual and the physical are created from God's energy. Everything is energy. It is energy in different forms. The higher the vibration, the closer to God's original form of pure energy. The lower the vibration, the more implanted the energy is in matter. There is no ethical consideration about this. What has been made manifest in physical form is as much a part of the power and love of God as the purely spiritual.

God loves all things. It is up to us as a species to learn to love God in return. We are all blessed with the flow of energy from God. It is our responsibility to learn to use it consciously and beneficially in our creative process. We can learn to bring love into our system and to send it out to others. This demands personal cleansing so that the love is not deflected by other vibrations we have stored in our body.

We are here on Earth to learn how to create with God's energy. We are like children who have been given a school in which to learn the creative principles of the Cosmos. We are meant to develop the creative power of God and to return this power freely to the Source. It is like children being sent out into the world to learn and grow, and then return to enhance the home with their experience and maturity.

We separate from the Source as pure energy, uninvolved with matter, to develop a separate consciousness. With this individual consciousness, we make decisions on our own. Some of the decisions we make are wise and some are foolish. Many spiritual beings give away most of their energy. Some beings take energy from others. All manner of games are played as we learn about manipulating the creative power of God's energy. This experience, outside of any type of body, has no ethics, only pure creative energy.

We get lost by forgetting that God is the Source of all things. We make our mistakes when we create without the conscious awareness of God. When we are in touch with God, our process is a continuous flow of creativity. When we are out of touch with our Source, we limit ourselves, our perspective and creativity, and we experience fear and doubt.

Eventually, we dissipate our original energy to the extent that we cannot return to our Source without re-gathering our original resources. We make agreements with each other or souls at the same level of development. We are much like teenagers who are out on a spree, who spend their money, and then have to pool their resources to return home. Planet Earth is one way we are pooling our resources as we learn our lessons and regain our energy.

We have made an agreement to work with each other and God to create and use planet Earth as a learning opportunity. We can practice creating and learning to gain strength and wisdom. The Earth is a manifestation of our spiritual energy in matter. How we create in this environment shows our level of spiritual maturity.

When we create in agreement with God's plan for us, we create beauty and harmony. When we create in competition with God, we create evil and disharmony. In establishing the structure on Earth, we worked with the formation of matter until we created a body that is appropriate to our purpose. In this process, many souls became engulfed in matter and forgot God. Many forgot they are spirit and now identify totally with the physical creations. Many souls on Earth are presently in this state of spiritual unconsciousness. The Godforce energy entering the Earth at this time is creating a high vibration and waking many sleeping souls. Some are awake and joyful, while others are afraid of the high energy. Some awaken reluctantly while others fight the spiritual wake-up call.

The energy from God is neutral. It does not have any consideration of what we call good or evil. Everyone is loved and assisted by God. We humans have altered God's energy in the Earth with our separation from God and our creation of good and evil as a control system to substitute for God. We are able to use energy in God's neutral manner. We are like children given clay to mold. Some of us mold works of art from the clay, some eat the clay, some throw it at others, some wish the clay were plaster. We have the freedom to do what we wish with this powerful creative energy. We can eventually learn to create in harmony with God instead of in competition.

The phenomenon of freewill was established by God in the original plan since we must return to God from our free choice. We cannot reach maturity by being forced. We have to choose to take responsibility for ourselves and our creations. To develop to the level of spiritual maturity that we seek, we have to choose every step of the way ourselves. We cannot develop if we are coerced by an outside force. We develop and regain our energy by choosing to do so of our own free will.

We have to overcome the complexity we have created in the body to achieve our spiritual freedom.

The intellect is one aspect of being engulfed in matter that confuses us a great deal. The intellect is part of the body experience. It is meant to be used to comprehend the physical world and all that is in it. If the intellect is filled with unnecessary information, the soul creates through that debris and makes life complex. We can spiritually clear the intellectual debris and create a simpler way of relating to the physical world.

Even when clear, the intellect cannot completely comprehend the spiritual realm. The body is like a computer, and the intellect operates from the data contained in this live computer. When a soul depends on the intellect for all of its information, it becomes separate from its spiritual nature and God. Doubt becomes its daily fare, and fear develops from this doubt. We need to learn to use the intellect to comprehend the physical reality and to transcend it to relate to our spiritual reality.

If a soul attempts to make all of its decisions from an intellectual perspective, it is limited to the body's view. This limited view cannot comprehend the unlimited power available to the soul. The intellect can block the understanding of freewill and personal responsibility. It tries to make its own choices in order to create through the data it contains. The soul gets overwhelmed by doubt and fear when it becomes engulfed in the intellectual process. The soul begins to intellectualize instead of know and see: "Why is this happening? How can I explain that? Whose fault is this?" Since the intellect cannot comprehend God, it cannot explain most of life's experiences.

The intellect rebels against the soul's total responsibility for its own decisions about how to create with God's energy. The intellect wants to understand everything, or in other words, wants to be God. The old story goes that Lucifer was lost because of his competition with God. It must be a true story since we have so much evidence in our own lives of the same experience.

The body and its intellectual perspective is not evil. Nothing is inherently evil. Everything depends on how we use it, including the intellect and all aspects of the body. All energy is originally from God. We must depend on faith or a spiritual knowingness to realize this and act upon it. Our body and the intellect can be used beneficially and creatively. Everything we have can be used in a spiritual manner. We can also get so lost in matter or the body that we forget we are spirit creating our world.

We have come from God. We have the constant flow of God's energy with which to create. We can create beauty and harmony in our body and life, or we can create misery, pain and evil. The choice belongs to every soul. We have all experienced choosing that which does not make us happy. We have all experienced being joyous about our choices. With the realization that we are spirit, we can regain conscious control of our creativity and create in agreement with God.

By creating as spirit, we regain our original level of energy. With this unique energy, we are able to draw our vibration out of the matter of the body and the Earth. This release of matter gives us the freedom to return to our Source. We created the matter of Earth and our bodies to regain our energy. We forgot we are spirit and part of God. We have put our attention on Earth and the body perspective to the point we forgot who we are and from whence we come. It is now time to remember who we are and awaken to our spiritual nature.

As each soul wakes up and remembers, the energy of the Earth is raised. The heaviness of matter lightens around us, and we are able to see more of the spiritual reality. When we take a step forward in spiritual awareness, we have to remember that, at this point in development, we must relate to our bodies. Until we leave the body completely, we must relate to the body as our creative vessel and learn to raise its vibration so we can flow through it.

This means that we have to learn how to spiritualize the body. The higher we are able to bring the vibration in the body, the more we are able to use the body for our spiritual purpose. Meditation is the safest and easiest way to raise the physical vibration to accommodate our spiritual energy.

Meditation allows us to move above the body's intellectual noise and experience ourselves as spirit. Through meditation, we can experience our spiritual purpose and relationship with God. The higher vibrations move through the body bringing it up to a level where we can use it more easily. We, as spirit, remember how to bring our energy to a level where we can relate to our body in harmony.

This cleansing and energizing process creates enormous growth in the soul and the body. Both vibrations have to adjust to the changes. The growth of the body is the most dramatic since this is what we experience in our conscious life. When the higher spiritual vibrations move through the lower body energy, they stimulate anything in the body that is not in harmony with the higher energy.

This is when we realize that pain, fear, hate and doubt are not in affinity with the higher vibrations of spirit. We quickly become aware of these and other debilitating energies we have created and stored in our bodies. This makes us look at what we have created. Some of our creations are not pleasant. We have to take responsibility for them and let them go to make room for our spiritual energy.

A lack of personal responsibility is one of the strongest blocks to experiencing your communion with God. When you seek the Oneness and, in the process, discover your mistakes, you often turn away to avoid facing your creative process. This puts you in competition with God. You attempt to do things your way instead of flowing with the energy of God. This way of operating gets you more engulfed in matter and less aware of spirit.

Personal responsibility puts you in harmony with God and your body. You acknowledge what you have and are creating and own that it is yours. By owning your creations, you can change them. If you do not take responsibility for your creations, you deny what you are doing and lose sight of your reality. When you do not take responsibility for your creations, you use your energy to create lies to protect your ego. By being responsible for your creations, you work in harmony with God, your body and everyone else. You can work with God when you act as a responsible creator.

As we learn to look to God, we also have to look to ourselves and our bodies. We need to clear from the body whatever would block our relationship with God. By consciously using the constant flow of energy from God, in a spiritual manner, we can cleanse what we need to and increase the vibration of the body. The more we use cosmic energy consciously, the more we see ourselves and what we need to cleanse as well as what we want to enhance. At first, it seems overwhelming. As you persevere, the process becomes a joyous way of life.

We are meant to have bodies of light. When we clear the denser vibrations from ourselves and bring more spiritual levels of energy into our bodies, these bodies of light shine. We can use our energy best by healing ourselves to let in more light. We have to learn not to judge our creations in order to heal ourselves. Judgement blocks the flow of energy because it takes our attention and stops motion.

Light is one way many people allow themselves to be aware of God. Light is a form of energy. Light is a beautiful and powerful aspect of God's energy flow. Some people try to determine what color of light or what vibration best represents God so they can use that color to be closer to God. God is all things and thus all light. If there is a color that best represents God, it is crystal clear light. Crystal clear light reflects all light spectrums. Just as a quartz crystal reflects color, so God's clear light contains all vibrations of light. White light is not the same as crystal clear light or what most people believe it to be. White light is the crystal clear light immersed in matter. The denser, slower vibration makes the white easier to see and to understand intellectually. White light can be used for protection in emergencies and to raise the vibration of colors. It is not beneficial to send white light to another person since it can freeze their energy and cause them to be afraid. Crystal clear light better represents Godforce energy as it reflects all light and is in motion.

All light is an aspect of God and can be used for spiritual work. It is more important how you use light than what light you are using. If you are projecting light to someone else, as in praying for someone, you may not be acting in a beneficial manner. The other person needs to want your prayers or you are invading their spiritual space and disrupting their energy. It is helpful to ask the soul verbally or telepathically if she wants your prayers and light. If you send light to someone wishing them harm, this will eventually return to you in some form. Everything you put out comes back to you.

Light is most beneficially used in your own space. You can consider your body and the energy just around it as your personal space. Using light as a way of healing and increasing your awareness and communication with God can be very helpful. In your meditations, you can use all of God's light spectrum. You can use various forms of light to do different things. If you need to be neutral, you will find gold light beneficial. If you are healing your body, you may find orange, blue or green energies soothing. If you believe one form of light is good and another is bad, you will limit your access to light. All light can be used to create and heal.

Love is another vibration through which we can experience God. There is so much confusion about what love is that we have forgotten it is a powerful vibration to communicate with God. Love is something everyone seeks. Few people are willing to find it since love is demanding and powerful. Love is an aspect of God. Love is energy. Love is a great power that we can learn to use.

Everyone has heard that love is God, but few understand this. Love, like God, has been humanized to the point of the absurd. Love is not control, sex or other body levels. God is not an old man with a beard in the sky. Love is spiritual energy. God is spiritual energy. Love can be translated into a vibration which we can receive and send. By using this vibration of love, we experience God.

Love is of the spirit and can be translated into the physical world. Love can be expressed through the body in many ways. Love can be experienced in all of the chakras in the spiritual system and in every cell of the physical body. It is most apparent in our physical reality in the first, fourth and fifth chakras which relate to reality, affinity and communication.

Love of God is the central issue for us all. We have to learn to love God above all else in order to return to God. If we focus on God, everything in our lives falls into place. If we are physically focused, we experience effort, frustration and struggle which is not necessary.

To love God, you must first learn to love yourself as a part of God. Once you experience your love moving from and to God within you, you can express it on every level of your creativity. Loving yourself and those around you is a powerful way of expressing your love of God. The love comes from God and needs to return to God to create a full circle. When this occurs, God is made manifest in the world.

One form of God is love. We cannot limit either God or love to physical terms. Love is not actions although it can be displayed through actions. We experience God in our daily life through this vibration of love. Love can be experienced silently within and can be actively shared with the world around us when we have it within. We bring this vibration of love into the Earth when we allow it in ourselves.

Good works are not required to be Godly. We are already a part of God. One can display love in an infinite number of ways including silent meditation. When we turn within and discover the joyous silence of God, we can display it outwardly in our own unique way. Some people display their love through their work, some through family interaction and others through their beingness in every way. Regardless of what you do, you can do it lovingly. Whether you are pouring concrete, cooking, tending a garden, nursing someone, meditating, teaching or doing anything or nothing, you can do it with the vibration of love. You can sit in silence and transmit the cosmic vibration of love to the Earth and to all in it.

God is a spiritual reality we all need to embrace. Love is a vibration through which this force flows easily. It requires strength to embrace God and experience love for we must face all of our creations to do this. We have to cleanse fear, hate, jealousy and other body energies to make room for the vibration of love. It is often difficult to accept these things in ourselves, but we must in order to clear them. It is infinitely freeing when we do heal and begin to let go of these limiting energies and fill ourselves with the freedom of the vibration of love.

We create space for the spiritual vibrations as we cleanse the physical energies. We can let go of our obsession with our ego and create spiritual freedom. By letting go of what is not important, we can see ourselves as a part of the Cosmic Consciousness. We see that everyone experiences God in his or her own way. Through experience, we learn that God is sufficient unto Itself. Our physical reality is no longer the significant factor. The silent, internal communication brings us the force and power of God's vibrations, by which we can shape our lives.

Each of us is a cell in this Cosmic Body. We are all able to communicate with every other cell and with the Creator. By turning within, we can contact all things including God. While in a body, we can do this most easily through the vibrations of love and light. We can do this by learning to know ourselves as spirit. We can use love and light by learning about our chakra system and balancing our sixth and fourth chakras which relate to clear sight and affinity. We have the information and need to remember who we are and how much we know.

When you balance your use of love and light, God manifests within and you experience your place in God's creation. Be still and know yourself as a part of God, and your reality becomes clear to you. Do not be afraid of the things you do not like about yourself. Let them go, forgive yourself and move on. God has already forgiven you.

Fill your newly created space with love and light. Do not be afraid about what to do with your new energy. God's flow of energy will direct you. This is one of the most difficult aspects of spiritual awakening: to take all of the power, strength and awareness you gain from God's energy and freely return it to God. To reunite with the Whole, after experiencing your own individual power, is spiritual maturity.

This desire to reunite with God is a major reason we must constantly heal ourselves to clear the debilitating energies such as fear and doubt. When we experience the power of God, we need to avoid using it to satisfy our own ego. This is where so many lose their path. They open, unfold, experience the power and begin to believe they alone are God. They lose track of the fact that we are all a part of God.

God is everything. Everything is God. Each of us is part of God. All we need to do is allow our communication and life takes on new meaning. Life is no longer a survival game but a game of spiritual growth and creativity. Life becomes an opportunity to choose God every minute of every day in thought, action and silence. It is important to remember that when we fall short of this, we are always forgiven. We simply need to forgive ourselves.

God has given us everything including the freedom to choose or deny God. It is up to us to grow toward this unity rather than away from it. By consciously using the energy of God to cleanse, communicate and create, we move along our path to reunite our vibration with God.

"A Walk and Talk With God"

I took a walk the other day,
Perched close on a branch was a hawk.

Why are you showing me this hawk, God?
Because the hawk is ever aware of his surroundings,
Be aware of what is going on around you.

Walking further, I saw a bush tit flittering in the reeds.

Why are you showing me this bush tit, God?
Because he is always in action,
Everything is constantly changing.

I saw an eagle with wings spread wide gliding on the air.

Why are you showing me this eagle, God?
Because the eagle is strong and beautiful,
You too are these things.

I saw a flock of crows cawing in the trees.

Why are you showing me these crows, God?
Because you think hawks and eagles are better than
crows,
But I love *all* my children.

Gail Coupal

UNIQUE PERSONAL VIBRATION

Every soul has a unique vibration. You may relate to this as a note in a symphony, or perceive the uniqueness as color in a work of art. Another way of conceiving of this is as a formula in a larger pattern. However you wish to relate to your unique vibration, the important thing is validating its significance.

You are unique and vibrate in a manner not replicated by any other thing. There is not another in the "mind" of God that is exactly like you. The most important thing for you to do is to manifest your unique vibration to the fullest extent possible.

When you vibrate at your unique level, you add to the Cosmic Symphony. If you do not discover and play your note, the entire Cosmos misses your unique vibration. This expression of your unique energy is the main reason you were created. You are meant to add to the intricacy and beauty of the Cosmos. By separating from your Source, you were able to develop a new level of creativity. The ultimate goal is to take this creative level and unique vibration back to the Source.

Many question why the One God who is perfect would want change. The reality is that God is energy and in constant motion. There is always change and growth. God is not static. While God appears to us to be changeless because God is infinite and immortal, God is actually in constant motion. We are a small part of the creativity of God. We are so small, in comparison, it is difficult for us to see the motion of God. We can see the motion in some aspects of God such as the movement of the planets and stars, but we do not notice the turning of the Earth because it is so much larger than our bodies and so close.

We must remember that we are a unique creation of God and are meant to express our own vibration to fulfill our purpose. Every part of God is important and every part is in motion. We must learn to express and create through our energy and clear anyone else's vibration so we can be unique and continue our personal dance. Movement and change are a natural part of our spiritual nature.

Every soul has encountered difficulties in its expression of self. A "spiritual story" may help us understand our need for our unique expression. In the beginning of our existence as separate consciousness, we began to experiment with our power and creativity. While manifesting as spirit without form, many lost the awareness of the importance of our unique vibration and our goal of growing and returning to the Source. We played games of giving away our energy, trading energies with other beings, taking energy away from others and making agreements with other beings. Many of these games were not beneficial to our purpose of learning and maturing. These games finally put many beings in a state of confusion and depletion.

We were confused to the point that we had to create a way to regain our energy and sort out what belonged to whom. We decided to manifest in matter to help us focus our attention so we could regain our energy. With the agreement and assistance of the Cosmic forces, we created planet Earth as an environment in which to learn, and create. Through this creative manifestation of spirit into matter, we planned to learn our creative lessons to regain our energy and reunite with God.

Unfortunately, we continued to play the same games of trading, making foolish agreements, invading and being invaded. Once we had manifested in matter, it was easy to allow the matter to take precedence over spirit. Instead of solving our problems, we complicated them by entrenching our mistakes in the form of matter. We continued to compete with God instead of being guided by our Source.

Fortunately, there were beings among us who did not lose the spiritual perspective. These beings maintained the spiritual information for everyone. There were also great teachers sent to us to help us remember that we are spirit learning to create. There were also volunteers from other realities who came to teach us and help us. With this help and guidance, we began to awaken again.

This story can help you understand how the loss of your unique vibration can disrupt your spiritual progress. The loss of the unique vibration of enough souls can disturb the development of an entire planet of souls. By owning and using your personal vibration, you make the entire human experience work more smoothly. When all souls vibrate in their own way, the whole works in harmony just as a symphony creates together while each part creates separately.

Even though we make so many mistakes with our gifts, God continues to love and help us. We are meant to learn difficult lessons and God is patient. In our struggle to learn, we forget our spiritual nature as we move deeper into matter and manifest in bodies on the

Earth. We then play our childish games through the bodies. We give up seniority to the bodies and the Earth and forget we are spirit. We get caught in the competition games we created soon after our spiritual birth. Souls do learn and gain their freedom, but the majority are still engulfed in matter and the physical games we have come to believe are important.

Approximately every two thousand Earth years, God creates an opportunity for those who wish to withdraw their energy from the matter of Earth and return to God. There is always a great teacher associated with this time. We also have a large number of visitors from other realities. Some come to observe and others to help those who can receive it. These are times of very high energy. The population of the Earth is greater than it was previously. This increase in the population is an opportunity for every soul to have as much energy in Earth as possible, so he can withdraw it when the energy is highest.

The way you can use this opportunity is by learning to know yourself. All of your spiritual information is stored in or can be accessed through your body. By getting to know yourself and manifesting your unique vibration, you can return to the freedom of the spiritual state. The soul is then senior to matter and able to create within matter or leave it, without loss. From this state of spiritual freedom, a soul can return to God or return to matter to assist other souls who have not found their freedom.

By experiencing your unique spiritual vibration and manifesting it, you have the freedom and power to create. When you realize that you are not encumbered by physical limits, you can consciously create your life on a spiritual level. All that you need to know to do this is within you. Through meditation, you can achieve this self-knowledge.

Enlightenment is being yourself. You are a unique vibration of God. Your body is a physical manifestation of your beliefs and vibration. You are meant to cleanse your concepts and get to the core vibration which is you as spirit. You have to take back the energy you have given away and give back the energy you have taken from others. You have to complete or end all of the agreements you made on Earth. You have to overcome the pull of the physical body and any ego you have created. You have to clear away all of the debris you have collected and get to the core light that is you.

This may appear to be an insurmountable list of things to accomplish, but it can be done. One has many lifetimes to do this work. There are many bodies for every spirit. We have many lives to regain our energy and remember our unique vibration. We not only have reincarnation to allow time for our growth, but most souls also manifest in more than one body in any single period of time. One may have a body in England and another in India, using both to learn spiritual lessons. This use of time and space helps us to learn, grow and mature.

This time on Earth is especially important for all of us since it is one of the two thousand year periods of spiritual awakening. There are hundreds of books being written on spiritual issues. There is information pouring in about meditation, healing, communication with the spiritual realm, the existence of extraterrestials, earth changes and much more. All of this is to help humanity wake up and take advantage of this important opportunity. The vibration of planet Earth increases at these times, and it is increasing a great deal during this transition. The high vibration gives us the opportunity to manifest more as spirit and to communicate more with the spiritual realm. A door is opening for us, and we must choose to move through it.

The easiest way to use this opportunity is to meditate and learn to know yourself. By manifesting your original vibration, you manifest your aspect of God. You can easily experience your vibration in the physical body through enthusiasm. You can regain your enthusiasm by meditating. When you feel enthusiasm, you are experiencing your God self. This spiritual excitement translates into the body and can manifest a feeling of joy, peace and euphoria.

Enthusiasm is one way to experience your unique vibration. When you feel enthusiasm, you are experiencing yourself. Being yourself is the way to fulfill your spiritual purpose of manifesting God within. This is, of course, a challenge since most every aspect of your world teaches you to be something other than yourself. The media, school, peer group, family, church and other organizations portray and dictate how you should act, look and be. You are seldom encouraged to look within to discover your own answers.

We have become so enamored and engulfed by the matter we created that we allow it to hold and enslave us. We have created societies which teach us that everything physical and outside ourselves is more important than we are. We are taught to be everything but ourselves. We are taught to copy the behavior of others, to fit in and to avoid being different. This program to focus outside self and avoid being unique gets in the way of achieving our spiritual goals.

Every soul has a unique vibration and a unique way of manifesting that vibration. We have to relearn the importance of our differences and uniqueness. The significance of the individual vibration is like the importance of different functions for body parts. The eyes are as important as the feet, and they fulfill very different functions. Each of us as spirit fulfills a different spiritual purpose through our own vibration.

Any machine, body or other physical thing has various parts that work together to make the whole function. The Cosmic Consciousness also has various energies that vibrate together to make the Whole. Each of us as spirit is one of those vibrations or parts that makes the Whole.

For anything to function efficiently in the physical world, it needs space. The world of matter requires time and space. When we manifest in matter, when we create through a body, we need space to function effectively. Each cell in a body is separate yet works in unison with the other cells. Every cell requires its own separate space to work. If the cells merge, this merging creates what we call cancer. When merged, the cells no longer function properly. This need can be observed throughout physical reality as in trees requiring space to grow properly and animals needing space to survive.

This is also true for us as spirit when we are in a body. We require space to manifest our unique vibration and our own concepts. When in a body, if we merge with another soul, we start manifesting that soul's vibration, concepts and physical reality. If we are trying to solve another's problems, we do not solve our own. By trading energies, we become confused about ourselves and cannot vibrate in our own way.

There is a great deal of misunderstanding about this issue of space. The powers that want souls caught in matter encourage merging or a cancerous state. They teach people to become one. Since spirit yearns for the Oneness experienced with God, it is easy for people to believe this is true. We have to remember that we were created as a separate consciousness for a purpose, and to fulfill that purpose, we need our God-given separate space.

To experience and manifest our unique vibration, we need personal space. We have to learn what is ours and what is not and clear what is not from our space. This clearing process includes letting go of the energy of our loved ones as well as of our enemies. Everyone has a right to space, even the people we love.

We are a part of God, not the totality of God. When we pull another's vibration into our space, or move our vibration into another's space, we are trying to play God, or we are trying to return to God in an impossible manner. We long for our union with God, so often we try to manifest that oneness with other souls like ourselves. This is a waste of time and energy since we have to separate from them and continue with our own growth to eventually be reunited with them in God.

This does not eliminate interacting with other souls. We are like the cells in a body, constantly interacting and supporting one another. We, like cells, must maintain our personal space to maintain a healthy "spiritual body." When we have our space and allow others to have their space, we are able to work together in harmony. With space, each soul is able to vibrate in its unique fashion and enhance the well being of all others.

We can see this on a larger scale in the world around us. When each person is allowed respect for individual space, each can fulfill her potential. This is true of family units, communities, religious and cultural groups. When each is respected and allowed to provide a unique contribution, the world is a rich and wonderful tapestry of light.

We are not meant to be alike. We are meant to be unique. This uniqueness provides immense beauty and experience. The opportunity for learning is enhanced whenever we allow the differences. God created us to learn, grow and add to the beauty of the Cosmos. With God, we created the body of Earth and our physical bodies to help us learn our lessons and create as spirit. The more we allow our unique vibration and create through it, the more we fulfill our purpose in the Cosmic Pattern.

There are many ways you can create your space and allow others their space. One is to respect the differences of others. Anyone can learn to let go of judgement of others. You need to realize that you are judgemental and then stop yourself every time you judge. You can change your pattern of judgement to one of acceptance by simply being aware of your behavior and substituting acceptance for judgement. Since you cannot have your space until you allow others their space, clearing judgement is a beneficial pattern to change early in your development.

You can also learn to establish and maintain your personal space through meditation. By turning within and learning to know your personal vibration, you know what to discard and what to keep. It is easier to maintain your space when your body and the space surrounding your body are filled with your vibration.

Amusement helps you accomplish this because amusement makes everything work smoothly and easily. You are healthier in every way when you take things lightly. Your amusement lets you be enthusiastic about yourself, your lessons, goals and life experiences. You can create without effort when you are amused.

You are a healthy cell when you are vibrating at your own rate within your space. Being yourself is the way you manifest God within you and within your surrounding environment.

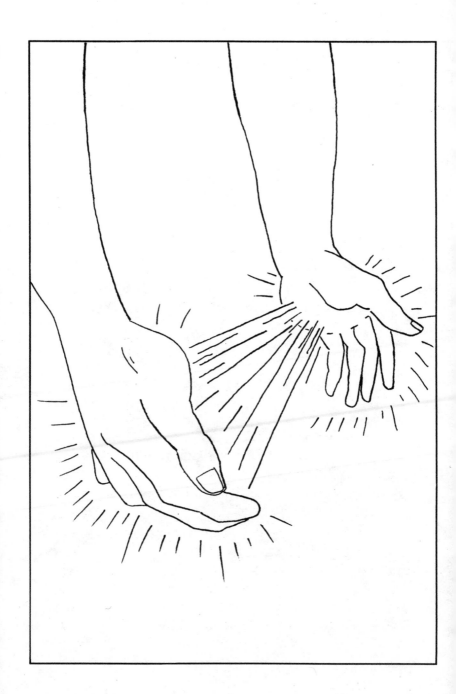

Healing and Creative Energies

Healing and creative energies are forms of cosmic energy. Any cosmic energy can be used in a healing or creative manner. We can experience these energies as vibrations, as colors, as an idea or concept, or as a state of being. A vibration is energy moving rapidly, and a state of being is energy moving slowly. While vibration is pure energy, a state of being involves the body and is a slower energy flow.

You can use vibrations to heal by visualizing the energy flowing to where you want it. You do not need to see a color or have a specific concept. You can simply allow a healing vibration to flow to the necessary space to have a healing effect. If you have a spiritual rather than a physical problem, you can use cosmic energy to help with that. In meditation, you can use vibrations to cleanse your system and heal your relationship with this or any reality. Cosmic energy can flow through your system without you having to be conscious of the details of the vibration. You only need to indicate that you want a vibration that is healing to you and your particular need.

For example, if you have a physical problem, you can allow healing energy to flow to the problem area. You can bring healing energy into a broken arm or a sore throat to help your body heal. You can also bring cosmic energy into your spiritual system, such as into a chakra, to heal your relationship with your body. You can allow the cosmic energy to flow into the chakra to help it turn smoothly and to cleanse it.

If you prefer to be more physically aware of what energy you are using, you can visualize the color of the vibration. You do this by using your clairvoyance or spiritual sight. For example, if you have an injured knee, you can visualize a clear light blue energy flowing to the injury and filling it with blue light. You can allow the blue energy to soothe and heal the knee. You can also use a gold, orange, green or any other color that feels comfortable to your body. Working with vibrations as colors for healing can be fun and beneficial. By allowing yourself to translate the vibration into a color, your body has more of a sense of participation in the healing process. The greater the cooperation from the body, the easier the healing process.

An idea or concept makes the healing vibration even easier for the body to understand. By conceptualizing the vibration, you have more intellectual comprehension of the healing process. If your knee is injured, you can get the concept of healing the knee. You can see the knee as whole and healed. You can also have the idea that whatever caused the injury is released from you so you do not recreate the injury. You can combine this with the visualization of color flowing into the area to create a powerful healing.

Another way of translating healing energy to the body is through a state of being. Emotions are the way the body talks to us as spirit. Emotions are a body form of energy. When we learn to master the emotions, we can use them to heal ourselves. As spirit, we can learn how to understand and use our emotions in a healing manner. By manipulating our emotions and healing energy, we can create a desired state of being. If you are experiencing fear, you can release it by using a healing vibration to cleanse the energy causing the fear. By releasing the fear, you can create a more peaceful state of being which will enhance healing.

You can learn to translate vibration into a state of being to enhance your healing. You can draw in a healing vibration, translate it into a color such as light blue and interpret the color as a healing state of being. You can learn to manipulate cosmic energy in a manner to heal you and your body.

Your healing is a process, not an isolated event. You will continue to discover energy that is not yours or is inappropriate and remove it from your system. By cleansing the energies you do not want, you create room for the vibrations you want. Healing yourself is similar to cleaning house. It is a continuing process that can bring satisfaction and exciting results. The more you heal, the easier it is.

You are spirit and can manipulate all manner of energy to create what you want. You can use energy on the unseen spiritual level and on the seen physical level. You have the spiritual ability to bring cosmic energy into your body and use it through your body to the point where you can project the cosmic energy from your body. Everyone projects physical energy, such as emotions and words. You can also learn to use cosmic energy as consciously as you do physical energy.

Since everything is energy, it is simply a matter of deciding what you want and then focusing your attention on it. If you desire healing and believe you can have it, you will create healing. The energy of healing will flow to and through you in every possible way. The people, things, and experiences you need will come to you through your desire and belief. Because there is an equal reaction for every action, your desire for and belief in healing will begin a chain of events or energy vibrations which will create healing.

You can create with cosmic energy in any area of your life. You can create physical things or spiritual experiences. You can use cosmic energy to make what you want manifest in the physical world. All you need to create as spirit is the desire for the creation and the belief that you can have it. You do need to be aware that you are responsible for what you create. You also need to remember that when you create with cosmic energies, you will receive what you send. If you create trying to be better than someone else, then eventually someone will be better than you. If you create hate, you will receive hate; if you send love, you will receive love.

Energy flows both to and from you, so when you create, you need to be aware of how you are using the cosmic energies that you receive. You may desire to create a more aware state of consciousness and believe you can do this. Your desire would start the process of energy flowing to you from the Cosmic Consciousness. This cosmic energy would begin to cleanse your system of whatever blocked you from being aware. If in the process you judged something you were cleansing, you would stop the process. You would probably feel frustrated and angry and look for someone to blame for your problem. By focusing outside yourself, you would interfere even more with your desired result and probably use the cosmic energies improperly. In this growth process, you could choose to go forward and cleanse the block, and in your awakened state, let go of the judgement and enjoy your creativity. You could also go the other route and use the power you received to harm yourself or someone else instead of creating your original desire.

Our spiritual creativity has great power. We need to be aware that what we put out comes back to us. It may not return in this lifetime, but it will eventually come back to us to balance the energy. Cosmic energy is in balance, and we are a part of that balance. When we create imbalance, we eventually rebalance whether we are conscious of the process or not.

Ideally, the cosmic energy flows both from and to God. God gives to each of us without reservation. God simply is. We need to remember that we have to receive from and send to God to complete the circle. We can send the vibration of love to any aspect of God, whether it is God in another person or in a flower. When the energy circle is complete, energy flows freely to the body and through it in a creative, healing manner. Simply stated, what we put out, we get back; what we do unto others is done to us; for every action there is an equal reaction.

The phenomenon, that for every action there is an equal reaction can be seen in the personal and the cosmic experience. Personally, if you are feeling upset and mean and you project this outwardly, you will have something mean return to you. On a larger spiritual scale, this is called karma. What you create in one life returns to you in another life. What you put out comes back. This can occur in seconds or over millions of years.

Our species, the human race, is experiencing some of this karma in the violent Earth changes. We can heal this process by changing what we project. Instead of putting out violence and hatred, we can project love and compassion. This change would allow a gentler energy to return to us. We can change the world by changing ourselves. By sending kindness, we receive kindness. When we send hate, we receive hate. Whether we act as an individual or as an entire species, we get back what we send out.

In healing, we can only heal ourselves, so it is important to realize that we must begin within to heal. We can create in our own space but not through another soul's space. We can disturb that other soul's reality, but we cannot create our reality through them. We have to learn to bring the spiritual energy into and through our own body. We also have to learn how to use and work within a body. When we establish this internal focus, we find that we have immense power. This power can be used to create what we want instead of being victim to our mistakes or the errors of others.

Turn within to learn how you and the physical world you have created work. Meditate on what you as spirit desire, and develop the faith to manifest what you want. The healing and creativity will follow. You need to continue your personal cleansing so your body's fear of your spiritual power does not stop your growth. For example, there was a student who had been absent for several months. She appeared at a workshop, and I asked her about her absence. She said that she frightened herself after learning to meditate and create consciously because she created everything she wanted. Fortunately, she overcame her fears and continued to create and heal.

By healing yourself and creating as spirit in your space, you heal the planet. The planet is like your larger body, so when you heal and create, as you are meant to, you do your part for the Earth. By healing and creating as part of God in the Earth, you do your job in the Cosmos. Everything is within you. By turning within and using the cosmic energies to consciously heal and create yourself, you change everything.

Meditate on what you want to create and how you want to heal yourself. Meditate on increasing your faith or belief about manifesting your desire. By learning to manipulate cosmic energies, you can create what you want and heal yourself. All you need to do this is the desire to create and heal and the belief that you can. The cosmic vibrations and earthly experiences will follow miraculously.

Everything in the Cosmos is connected. Your use of cosmic energies makes you a conscious creator in the Cosmos. Your healing and creative energies can be used for you to create what you desire for yourself and through you for the world.

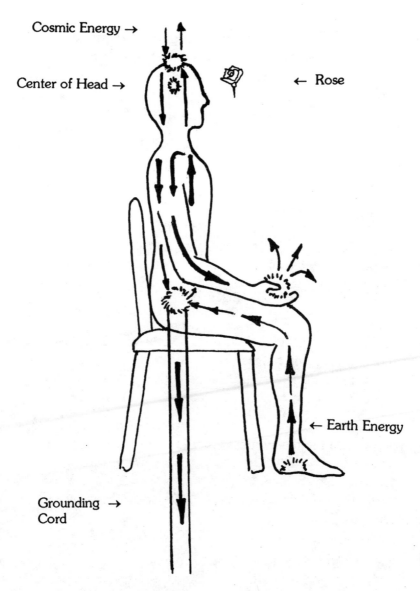

Cosmic Energy →

Center of Head →

← Rose

← Earth Energy

Grounding →
Cord

Figure1. Grounding, Center of Head, Running
Energy, Creating & Destroying a Rose

SPIRITUAL TECHNIQUES

Everyone is spirit. Everyone has spiritual abilities such as clairvoyance, telepathy and healing. We can use spiritual techniques to help us regain our spiritual abilities. These techniques and abilities assist us to know ourselves as spirit and to communicate with God. Our one-to-one communication with God is the most important thing. When we have this communication, life flows as it is meant to, and if we do not have it, we lose our way. Spiritual techniques help us focus on spirit and on God.

Everyone is a part of the Cosmic Consciousness of God. We have all come from the same Source. Whether one chooses to relate to God through a formal religion, or through personal methods, the goal is the same. We all need communion with God. A first step is realizing that we are spirit and part of God.

Spiritual techniques can help you find this communion. If you are involved in a formal religion, you can use the techniques to better serve your path. If you like to communicate with God in a private manner, you can also find these techniques beneficial. The techniques help you be aware that you are spirit and have spiritual abilities.

You are spirit. You are not your body. These spiritual techniques assist you to manifest as spirit in a body. You can take charge of your physical creations by grounding and focusing in the center of your head. You can learn to experience light and love in your body by using the techniques. You can learn to have your personal vibration and space to express it. The techniques assist you to manipulate cosmic energy to create your reality.

All of the information you have read can easily become meaningless to you if you do not find a way to experience and express it in your life. The meditation techniques that follow can help you live your experience of God. You can learn to use earth and cosmic energies which assist you to experience and balance your spiritual and physical realities. You can learn to consciously create on a spiritual level and how this affects your life. When you use spiritual techniques to meditate, you manifest yourself as spirit.

The techniques presented are: grounding, centering in your head, running earth and cosmic energies, creating and destroying as spirit, and the aura. Also included are spiritual creativity with mock-ups and meditation with color. Every technique offers a new perspective of you as spirit and new insight into how to manifest your spiritual creativity. These and other techniques are presented in the Key series, four spiritual textbooks listed in the front of this book.

Many people find they have difficulty quieting the intellect and focusing during meditation. These techniques give you a focus and help quiet the chatter of the mind. By practicing spiritual techniques, you are able to manifest the spiritual principles you believe. When you operate as spirit, you establish your spiritual seniority with your body and your creations. Meditation can help you remember how to be focused on God.

It is not enough to intellectually know of God. You must learn to manifest God in your life in every way possible to learn your lessons. These simple techniques can help you take charge of your body and creations so you can again be in communication and harmony with God.

You need a quiet place to meditate where you can close your eyes and not be disturbed for at least thirty minutes. You cannot experience meditation safely while driving a car or doing any physical activity. Your attention must be spiritually focused during meditation for you to get the greatest benefit from it. If you are focused on your physical world, you are not able to achieve a deep meditation state. The spiritual techniques require your participation rather than your intellectual attention.

Meditation is a great joy. Be patient with yourself, and you will eventually experience the peace and joy of communicating with yourself and with God.

To practice the spiritual techniques, sit in a straight backed chair in an upright position. Place your feet flat on the floor and your hands separate in your lap. Keep your spine as straight as possible as this helps your energy to flow more easily. Take a few slow, deep breaths to relax your body.

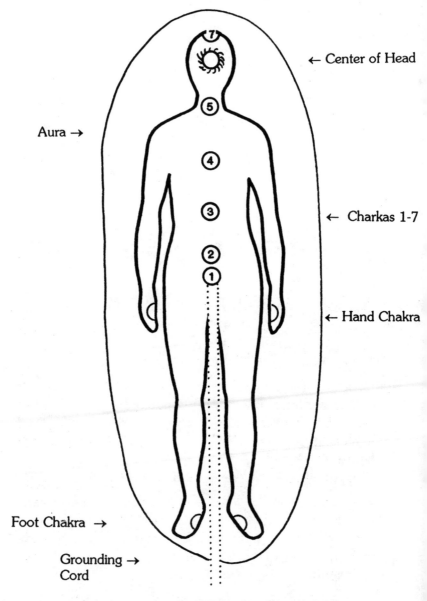

Figure 2. Grounding, Center of Head, Major
Chakras, Aura

GROUNDING

The spiritual technique of grounding is essential in all spiritual work. Grounding puts you in control of your creativity with cosmic energy. Grounding connects you as spirit to your body and to the Earth. You as spirit need to connect yourself to your physical reality to operate fully in it. If you are not grounded, you are not focused or committed. Without focus or commitment, you cannot accomplish your goals. You need to be grounded to focus on your body and your Earthly creations.

Grounding is the technique that allows you, the energetic spirit, to relate to your body. If you do not ground the body, it will become uncomfortable and disturbed when you operate through it. You are a much higher vibration than your body, so your body needs to be grounded as you move through it. If lightening strikes a house and it is grounded, the energy flows safely into the ground. If there is no grounding, the lightening can cause a great deal of damage to the house.

Your body is like your home. When you ground your home, you keep it safe and can use it effectively. Part of your lesson as spirit is learning how to use a body and how to operate in time and space. You have to learn how to operate within matter without losing your spiritual perspective and vibration.

Grounding is the first step in regaining spiritual seniority, since it puts you as spirit in charge and helps you operate through the body in a safe manner. Some people are naturally grounded while others have to put a great deal of attention on grounding to learn it. If you are not able to focus your attention, jump at loud noises, get frightened easily, have difficulty believing in yourself, then you are not grounded.

Grounding helps bring more of you as spirit into your body. This makes your body feel safe because you are there to protect and guide it. You can then make your decisions from a spiritual perspective instead of from a physical point of view. Grounding allows you to use the cosmic energies safely and effectively. Grounding also lets you release energy from your body and energy system. You can send energy that you do not want down your grounding cord.

**Sit straight in your chair with your feet flat on the floor and your hands separate in your lap. Breathe slowly and deeply a few times to relax your body.

**Be aware of your back leaning against your chair and your bottom sitting on the chair. Tune into your body and let it bring your attention into the present.

**Be aware of the energy center near the base of your spine. This is your first chakra. It contains your information about how to relate to the physical reality. You ground from your first chakra.

**Create a cord of energy flowing from your first chakra, near the base of your spine, to the center of the Earth. Take a few deep breaths and adjust to being grounded.

**Sit quietly and let energy flow down your grounding cord from your first chakra to the center of the Earth. Feel the stability your grounding provides.

**Take a few moments to experience your grounding cord. Be aware of how your body reacts to being grounded.

Grounding can also be used to release energy as well as to create a connection with your physical creations. As spirit, you collect energy. You do not want to keep all of this energy. Your grounding cord is one way of releasing excess or unwanted energy.

As spirit, you are constantly collecting data and using energy. You also take in data and energy from others. You need to release the foreign information and energy you have collected. You also need to release any unnecessary energy and data you have created. Grounding provides you with a safe, easy way of releasing energy.

**Sit up straight. Breathe deeply. Create your grounding cord from your first chakra, near the base of your spine, to the center of the Earth.

**Be aware of some information you accepted from someone else that you no longer want to keep. Release the data down your grounding cord. Take a deep breath and release any remaining energy.

**Notice any foreign energy you have in your body. You may experience it as tension. Release the foreign energy down your grounding cord. Use your breathing to help you release the energy down your grounding cord.

**Be aware of your body. Notice if you have more energy in your body than it is comfortable with in the present. Release any excess energy down your grounding cord.

**Use your grounding cord to release any information you no longer want to keep. For example, you may have an old belief that does not work for you in the present. Put your attention on the belief, and let it go down your grounding cord.

All of the energy you send down your grounding cord will be neutralized and reused. Energy is never destroyed, only recycled. Energy may change form, but it is not eliminated.

You can be grounded at all times, when you are awake and asleep, twenty-four hours a day. Grounding can assist you in any physical or spiritual endeavor. By grounding, you create a safe place in which to experience life, whether working, playing or meditating.

Grounding is the foundation of the spiritual techniques. Ground before you begin any spiritual work, including meditation, and you will create in harmony with your body and other physical creations. Your grounding creates safety and release for you during your spiritual journey.

CENTERING IN YOUR HEAD

You are spirit. Your body is your temple and your head is your throne room. In modern terms, your body is your airplane and your head is your cockpit. Either way, the head is the place to be in charge of your reality.

The physical and the spiritual eyes are in the head. To see clearly in this world, you must be in your head. The center of your head is where you can see and experience neutrality. When you are neutral, you do not have to judge your creations or others. You use time effectively when you do not waste time on judgement.

You as spirit are most easily seen as a bright light. You can manifest any place at any time. You can manifest into the center of your head. You can be anywhere in your body or out of your body. You are most certain, clear and aware in the physical world when you are in the center of your head.

To use cosmic energies effectively, it is helpful to be in the center of your head. From this neutral place, you can control what you are doing. You can see what you are creating and be neutral about it. You can change it if you wish. The center of your head is your place of control, clarity and neutrality when in your body.

**Sit quietly with hands and feet separated and spine straight. Create your grounding cord from your first chakra to the center of the Earth. Experience your grounding for a moment, to let your body adjust.

**Focus your attention into the center of your head. Let the bright light that is you be above and behind your eyes, in the center of your head. Take a moment to let your body adjust to having you there. Breathe deeply and relax.

**Increase the flow of energy down your grounding cord. You are more energetic than your body, so you need more grounding when you come into your body.

**Move from the center of your head to the top of your head. Move back into the center of your head.

**Move from the center of your head to the top of your head, and then move to three feet above your head. Be aware of being outside of your body.

**Move slowly through the top of your head, back to the center of your head. Take a few deep breaths, and relax your body.

**Release any unwanted energy down your grounding cord. Focus in the center of your head, as you release the energy, so you do not have to judge it.

Practice being in the center of your head often. You can be there at any time, while you are meditating, working, playing a sport, talking or doing anything. If you practice centering in your head, you will soon learn to operate from this neutral spiritual space. When you are in the center of your head, you are in charge of your reality.

CREATING AND DESTROYING AS SPIRIT

Creating and destroying roses is a technique we can use to reestablish spiritual seniority in our creativity. Most souls have allowed the body, ego and other influences to affect their creations to such an extent they no longer have control of them. Creating and exploding roses allows the soul to regain control and create what it wants instead of what the body or others desire.

Everything is energy and energy is constantly in motion. Change is one thing which is constant in all realities. You can take control of your personal creativity and change things according to your plan. You are meant to be the conscious creator of your reality. Creating and destroying roses helps you get back to this level of spiritual seniority.

The use of a rose in this technique is significant since the rose is a symbol for the emergence of the soul to God. The lotus is the Eastern symbol, and the rose is the Western symbol representing spiritual awakening. The rose is also a beautiful and neutral symbol to visualize.

Your clairvoyance, or ability to see spiritually, is located in the center of your head. You can use your clairvoyance to see a rose, as you create and destroy it, by focusing in the center of your head. Your clairvoyance gives you a neutral, spiritual perspective of your creativity.

One reason we are here on Earth is to learn about creativity. We as spirit need to learn how to create into and through matter. Creating and destroying roses is a spiritual technique we can use to practice our creative abilities. When we consciously take control of our creativity, we take a big step toward spiritual maturity.

Regaining your spiritual seniority can be exciting and fun. Use the rose symbol with neutrality and joy and allow yourself to enjoy your awakening. When you discover something you do not like, you can put it in a rose and destroy it.

**Sit up straight with your feet on the floor and hands separated in your lap. Breathe deeply and relax your body.

**Ground from your first chakra, near the base of your spine, to the center of the Earth. Take a moment to relax with your grounding cord.

**Focus your attention into the center of your head. Let your body adjust to having you there by increasing your grounding.

**Take a few deep breaths, and adjust to being in your head and being grounded. Say hello to your body, and give it time to adjust to your presence.

**From the center of your head, create the mental image picture of a rose in front of your forehead. Let it be about six to eight inches in front of your forehead. Admire your creation.

**Destroy the rose by letting it disappear, explode, melt, etc. Admire your ability to create change in the absence of the rose.

**Create another rose. Destroy the rose. Create and destroy roses, at your own rate, to practice the technique.

Creating and destroying roses helps you to get into the present with the rose symbol. It cleanses your energy system and softens your energy. It allows you to practice your God-given spiritual ability to create and destroy.

This technique can also be used to release energy from your body and spiritual system. You can put concepts, pictures, ideas and foreign energy into a rose and explode the rose. In doing this, you release the unwanted energy. You return energy that is not yours to its original source.

**Ground and center in your head. Create a rose in front of your forehead. Destroy the rose.

**Create a rose in front of you. Be aware of one belief you have that you do not want. For example, you may have the belief that you are unworthy. Put the unwanted belief into the rose, and explode the rose and the belief. Create and explode roses for this belief until you have let it go.

**Be in the center of your head. Increase your grounding. Create and explode a few more roses to clear your system.

You are changing the configuration of energy in your system when you create and explode roses. You are changing from one cosmic vibration to another. The vibration you have may be in the form of invalidation such as "you are unworthy." The change you create in your vibration by destroying the old concept can create a new form of energy such as "you are worthy."

An energy shift such as this can produce immense change in your life. If you go from feeling unworthy to feeling worthy, you will change your relationship with everything spiritual and physical. Manipulating cosmic energy is powerful and life changing.

Practice creating and destroying roses when you are grounding and focusing in the center of your head. You will eventually be able to explode roses in most circumstances. By creating and exploding roses, you avoid accepting unwanted ideas from others, and you clear your own unwanted concepts.

This spiritual technique can help you clear your space so you can communicate more easily with the spiritual realm and with God. It can assist you to maintain a clear energy field through which to operate. Spiritual seniority is a goal in spiritual opening. You gain seniority by taking conscious control of your creativity.

RUNNING ENERGY: EARTH AND COSMIC

All energy is cosmic energy. The Earth or physical world is made up of slow moving forms of cosmic energy. It is helpful to differentiate energies so we have a clearer view of our reality and how to work with it. We can divide energy into the categories of earth and cosmic.

Cosmic energy is the energy of the cosmos and earth energy is that part of the cosmos making up the matter of Earth. The vibrations of the cosmos are infinite. Some are slowed into matter and others are pure energy.

Earth energy is the spectrum of vibrations that make up the planet Earth. Some of the vibrations of Earth are seen and some are unseen. The spiritual energies we work with are the unseen vibrations. We can use them to heal, communicate and create. We are better able to work in harmony with Earth when we consciously use earth energy.

We use both earth and cosmic energies since we are manifesting as spirit in a body. We are spirit creating in and through matter. We need to use both the energy of spirit and the energy of matter: cosmic and earth. By using both energies, we are able to create on both levels. If we eliminate one or the other, we limit ourselves in our creativity. We will be caught on either the spirit or the body level unable to create on the other.

Some beings choose to operate on strictly spiritual or physical levels. A spiritually aware soul may decide to leave the body in a seemingly dormant state and operate outside of the body on an almost exclusively spiritual level. This is observed in India and in other cultures where spiritual work is respected. The other extreme is when a soul has no contact with spiritual reality and operates strictly on Earth principles. While no one completely eliminates cosmic or earth energy from their system, they can choose to minimize one or the other.

Ideally, we use a balance of both earth and cosmic energies. The cosmic energy is used in the upper system and the earth energy is used in the lower part of the system. The upper chakras or spiritual energy centers relate more to spiritual vibrations and the lower chakras relate to earthly vibrations.

By learning to use and manipulate both energies, you take charge of your experience on Earth. You can use the type of energy you need according to the situation. You may want to use more earth energy to help you ground in a frightening circumstance. You may want to use more cosmic energy while meditating and communicating with God.

Running earth and cosmic energies is an exciting spiritual exercise. You can learn to be in charge of your energy and its balance. You can manipulate these vibrations to enhance your life experience.

**Ground from your first chakra to the center of the Earth. Focus into the center of your head. Breathe deeply and relax.

**Create a rose in front of your forehead and explode it. Create and explode roses to help you clear your system.

**From the center of your head, be aware of the bottoms of your feet. There are energy centers in the arches of your feet called feet chakras. Allow earth energy to flow up through your feet chakras.

**Let the earth energy flow up through channels in your legs to your first chakra. Allow the energy to flow from your first chakra, near the base of your spine, down your grounding cord.

**Be in the center of your head and experience the flow of earth energy up through your feet chakras, through your leg channels, to your first chakra and down your grounding cord.

**Be still and enjoy the flow of earth energy for a few moments. Talk to your body about how it feels as you run this earth energy.

Earth energy helps you relate to the Earth and to your body. Your body is an aspect of the Earth and ideally will like earth energy. If your body has difficulty with earth energy, ground, center, and create and explode roses to release the disturbance that interferes with your relationship with Earth.

Earth energy can be comforting and healing. It is powerful energy and needs to be used gently. You can use earth energy at all times. You may want to use more at some times than others, such as when playing a sport or doing anything physical.

Cosmic energy is the infinite vibrations available to us from the Cosmic Consciousness. Cosmic energy has no limits. The only limit to your use of cosmic energy is your personal beliefs and the limits of manifesting through a body.

COSMIC ENERGY

Cosmic energy can be seen and experienced in a variety of ways. We use vibration to communicate through radio waves and to see by using light. Cosmic energy can be translated in many ways such as formulas, sound and color. The easiest way to experience cosmic energy is by translating the vibrations into color.

**From the center of your head, ground from your first chakra to the center of the Earth. Create a rose and destroy it to clear your space.

**Run your earth energy up your leg channels and down your grounding cord to stabilize your system.

**Be aware of the top of your head. There are energy channels that come into and go out of the top of your head at your crown chakra. Be still and feel this area.

**Let cosmic energy flow into the top of your head in the channels at the back of your head. Allow the energy to flow like water down channels on each side of your spine to your first chakra near the base of your spine.

**Mix the cosmic energy with earth energy at the first chakra. Move the mixture up through the channels that run along the sides of the chakras toward the front of your body. Let the energy run to the top of your head and out the top of your head.

**Move some of the cosmic energy from the cleft of your throat down channels in your arms and out of your hands and fingers.

**Be still and experience the cosmic energy flow through your system. Be aware of the earth energy balancing the cosmic energy flow.

You can use any vibration of cosmic energy. Practice with a variety of energies, and you will learn what is most healing for you in the present. You will increase your vibration as you run your energies, so you will find higher levels of energy more comfortable as you cleanse. Lower vibrations are helpful when working with body issues and while you cleanse the body to increase its energy. Lower vibrations are also comforting when the body is not feeling well.

The vibration level is easily determined through color interpretation. Brown is a lower vibration than red, and blue is a lower vibration than violet. Gold is a higher vibration than blue, and silver is a higher vibration than gold. The clarity of the color also determines the level of energy. If the color is dense, it is lower than when it is clear. When you add white to a color, it raises the vibration, and when you add more of the color, it lowers the vibration.

You can be in charge of the vibrations you run. You can raise and lower the vibrations. You can cleanse the colors of foreign and inappropriate energies to raise the vibration. You can lower the vibration to allow your body to be comfortable and to allow those around you to be comfortable. You can raise the energy to cleanse and to enhance spiritual communication.

Vibrations translated into color are our creative energies. Like a painter with a brush and palate of colors, we create our reality with these vibrations. We raise and lower our vibration and manipulate our energies to create what we want. We can create all levels of emotion with our changes in vibration.

We can also create an atmosphere within and around us with cosmic energies. Our ability to manipulate cosmic energy is our birthright. God has given us creative abilities so we can learn and grow to a level of spiritual maturity. Cosmic energy is the energy we use to create everything in our reality. Everything is energy, so our finances, our jobs, our relationships, our health, our happiness and everything in our lives is created from cosmic energy.

You can learn to manipulate cosmic energy to create what you want in your life. If you do not like your work, you can manipulate energy to create what you want. You can use cosmic energy to heal yourself. You can create your entire reality by consciously manipulating cosmic energy within your personal space.

You must learn some basic spiritual principles to do this. You have to create without effort and with faith. Your personal belief system will make it possible for you to create what you want or block you from your spiritual creativity. You can use the techniques to clear interference to creating with cosmic energy.

**Ground, center in your head, and run your earth and cosmic energies. Create and destroy several roses.

**Look at one belief interfering with creating with cosmic energy. Create a rose, put the block into the rose, and explode them both until they disappear.

You just created with cosmic energy. The rose and the belief were created with cosmic energy. You destroyed what you did not want, thus creating new space to create what you do want.

You create from your beliefs, thus you must believe that you can create with cosmic energy in order to do it.

**Create and destroy roses to cleanse your system. Use your grounding to let go of any other energies you wish to release. Creating and destroying roses and grounding are also ways of manipulating cosmic energy.

**Be in the center of your head, and enjoy the flow of earth and cosmic energies. By running these energies through your system, you are creating with cosmic energy.

**Bend forward and reach your hands to the floor to release energy from your head, shoulders and arms.

**Sit up and continue your meditation.

Cosmic energy is our creative power. We create as awakened spiritual beings by consciously using earth and cosmic energies to create our reality. We learn to balance our spirit-body dichotomy and to gain seniority over the body. We awaken the God Within when we use our creative power consciously.

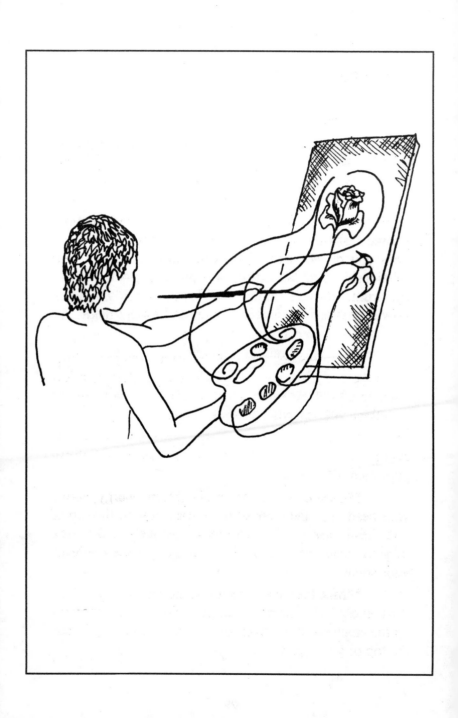

COLOR MEDITATION

You can use the infinite variety of cosmic energies to create your reality. The color meditation helps you learn how to use vibrations and how you personally relate to different energies.

Everyone is different, so you relate to energies in a unique fashion. You are aware of colors you like and ones you do not like. You can learn to cleanse your relationship with all color, so you can use the entire spectrum. By meditating on different colors, you learn how they affect you and how you can best use them.

**Always begin your meditation with grounding. Be in the center of your head. Create and destroy a few roses to clear your head. Refer to the preceding lessons to refresh your memory of these techniques.

**Run your earth energy. Run your cosmic energy. Refer to the "Running Energy" lesson to refresh your memory.

**Create a ball of bright green energy above your head. Let the clear green energy flow to the top of your head, into the cosmic energy channels in the back of your head, and down the channels on each side of your spine.

**Mix the clear green cosmic energy with your earth energy at your first chakra, and move the energies up the channels in the front of your body to fountain out the top of your head.

**Let some of the green energy flow from the cleft of your throat down your arms and out of your hands.

**Be in the center of your head and experience the vibration of green. Notice how your body responds to green.

**Translate the color green into some words that have meaning to you. Then see how you can use this vibration in your life.

You may want to use clear green to help you through times of change. You could use it as a soothing or healing energy. If you discover that this vibration has a soothing effect, you can use it any time you experience stress to relieve the disturbance. Every vibration has a different effect on you and those around you. By practicing with various cosmic vibrations, you learn what you like to use in different circumstances.

**Use your meditation techniques: ground, center in your head, create and destroy roses, run earth and cosmic energy.

**Create a ball of blue energy to replace the green energy, and run the blue through your system. Experience the energy and how your body relates to it. See how you can use this vibration in your life.

**Tune into how you already use blue energy. See other ways you can use this vibration.

**Allow time to run the blue energy to let your body adjust and respond to it. Translate the energy into words that have meaning for you.

After you have experienced the blue energy, do the same exercise with the following colors: red, orange, yellow, violet, purple, and pink. Take time to experience each color and its significance for you.

When you feel comfortable with those colors, run gold cosmic energy and let your body adjust to that vibration. See how you can use gold to heal your life. Gold can help you enhance your neutrality and raise the vibration of your body. When your body energy is higher, you can move into and through it more easily.

Use different vibrations freely. There is no correct color or vibration for you to use at all times, since you have the full spectrum available to you. You can learn to consciously change your vibration according to circumstance and need. For example, if you feel depressed, you may be running a vibration that is too low for you. You can run a higher vibration and raise your energy and your spirits. Keep a journal of your experiences, and you will learn a great deal about yourself.

Practice using a variety of vibrations translated into colors every time you meditate, and you will soon learn how to manipulate your reality using cosmic energy.

YOUR AURA: YOUR CREATIVE SPACE

The aura is the outward manifestation of your energies. The aura is the electromagnetic field around your body. Your aura emanates from your chakras. Your aura is a demonstration of the state of being of your spiritual system. When you learn to translate the vibrations of your aura, you learn to know yourself as spirit and how you are creating in the physical world.

Your aura is cosmic energy flowing through your chakra system. Different vibrations flow through and from each chakra even when you consciously adjust your system to use only one vibration. Each energy is a statement of what you are creating in the chakras. If you have a medium yellow color in the first layer of your aura, you may be intellectualizing your relationship with your body. By knowing this, you have the power to create your reality consciously. You can change the vibration or leave it the same with the knowledge of what you are creating.

Your aura is a constantly changing flow of energy. It is meant to be in motion and altering vibrations. There is not a static vibration or set of vibrations that is ideal for anyone. As you grow and change, you change your vibration and increase the amount of energy you are able to use. You may first see your aura as darkened or of lower vibrations than you see after meditating for some time. Your cleansing raises your energy.

As you meditate on your aura, you will recognize vibrations that you use often or even all of the time. Some healers use gold and blue energies frequently.

You may find some energies become a regular part of your vibratory repertoire. You will discover the vibrations in your chakras as you learn to use different energies for your creative process.

It is important to be aware of and consciously use your aura if you wish to manipulate cosmic energy. You have to be able to control your own energy before you can control other levels of energy. Start by getting to know your aura in the present. As you run your energies, see how your aura changes. As you become comfortable meditating, use the color meditation to help you cleanse and alter the energy in your aura.

**Be grounded, in the center of your head, and create and destroy roses for a moment.

**Run your earth and cosmic energies until you are comfortable with the energy flow.

**From the center of your head, be aware of your aura. Let it flow around your body. Allow the aura to be behind your back as well as in front of you and to come down under your feet.

**From the center of your head, experience your aura flowing around you. Be aware of it all around your body. See yourself, like the flame of a candle, with the aura glowing around it.

**As the cosmic energy flows out of the top of your head, be aware of it flowing through your aura. Allow it to flow all around your body.

**Move your aura under your feet. Create and explode roses to move the energy under your feet.

**Move your aura above your head, behind your back and all around you. Create and destroy roses to help the energy flow. Take a few deep breaths to help your energy flow. Let your aura be six to eight inches around you.

**Be in the center of your head, and experience the flow of your aura around you. Let the flow of cosmic energy cleanse your aura without effort.

Your aura is the outward flow of cosmic energy moving into and through your chakra system. It lets the world know your state of being. Your aura shows your emotions, affinity, clairvoyance and so forth in vibrations that anyone can translate into colors. By becoming consciously aware of your aura, you can take control of your use of cosmic energies and create your reality the way you want it to be.

You can run the infinite variety of cosmic energies through your aura to cleanse it. You can also direct different colors through your aura to change the vibration and consciously create your reality.

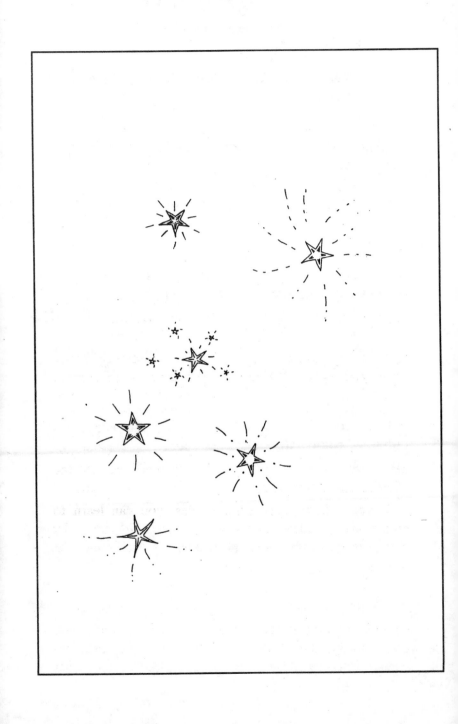

MOCKUPS: YOUR COSMIC CREATIVITY

You as spirit have the ability to create anything you want. Your only limit is your doubt. You can learn to consciously create on a spiritual level and manifest your creation in the physical world. A mock-up is one way to do this.

A spiritual mock-up is similar to a paste-up for a graphic artist. You create what you want on a spiritual level, and then clear any interference to manifesting it into the body. In a similar way, a graphic artist creates on the computer what he wants, and then prints it into the physical world.

Mock-ups can be used to learn to consciously create what you want. You can mock-up a job, more grounding, joy, money, a parking place or anything you want. There are a few rules that apply to mock-ups to make them work: the mock-up must fit into this physical reality, be in present time, be within what you can have (work in your belief system), be created without effort, and be released so it can return to you.

If you follow these simple rules, you can learn to create your reality the way you want it to be by manipulating cosmic energy. It does require faith in the process.

**Prepare to create spiritually by establishing your meditation state: ground, center in your head, create and destroy several roses, and run your earth and cosmic energy. Use a color of cosmic energy that enhances your creativity. Refer to the previous lessons to help you do this correctly.

    **From the center of your head, see what you want to create. For practice, start with something simple that is not emotional for you.

    **Create a rose in front of your forehead about six to eight inches. Put the thing you want to mock-up into the rose, and explode the rose to release interference from the mock-up. Explode the rose with the mock-up in it to let go of any effort and any beliefs that block the creation.

    **Continue to create and destroy the rose to release energy that is not in the present or that does not fit this reality.

    **When you have cleared interference to manifesting your creation, let the rose and the mock-up go. Visualize it like a balloon floating away from you until it is gone.

    **Create and destroy roses to clear your space to receive the creation when it returns.

    **Practice this technique often, and it will become easy and natural for you.

You can create anything in this manner. You can experiment with different color vibrations to discover which is your best energy level for different aspects of creativity. You may like a gold vibration to create spiritual mock-ups, or a clear red to create physical ones. Everyone is different. Allow and enjoy your uniqueness as you create as spirit. Ground, center in your head and use all of your spiritual techniques to help you be in charge of your creativity.

You are spirit, and you create your reality. Mock-ups help you create your reality consciously instead of unconsciously. It is time for spirit to awaken in this physical reality and begin to create consciously. It is a learning process, so allow yourself time and practice. Also, remember to release any fear of your creative power as your mock-ups manifest.

COSMIC ENERGY AND YOU

You are cosmic energy. You are a part of God. All things are made up of cosmic energy. You as spirit are vibrating rapidly. Your body is slow-moving cosmic energy called matter. You can learn to manipulate these energies to create your reality on a spiritually conscious level.

Meditation can lead you into yourself and your spiritual awakening. You can use your quiet, inward experience to learn about your spiritual power and how to manipulate cosmic energy to create and heal. You can use your spiritual abilities and energies to heal yourself and assist in the healing process of others. You can manipulate cosmic energies to create anything in your reality.

What do you want to create? You can create whatever you desire and believe. You can use the infinite power and flow of cosmic energy to consciously create your experience here on Earth. If you want material things, you can create them. Material creations give you practice with your creative process but do not necessarily help you develop your spiritual awareness. You can consciously create your spiritual awakening and development which brings an unending adventure.

You are meant to create with power and faith. God has given you the gifts of all spirit, to create as a god in human form. You have the ability to see spiritually, so you can unveil the spiritual mysteries and see beyond the physical world. You have the ability to communicate on every level; verbally, telepathically, over long distances, and with spirit not inside bodies. You can talk directly with the world teachers, with angels and with God.

You are a creator, a healer, a child of God. You have capabilities you can use to create your reality in a conscious, powerful way. You are not anyone's victim unless you create that for yourself. You are the creator in your body which is your universe.

Wake up to your spiritual self and God within you and within everyone. Let yourself see the bright spark of spirit, the colors of auras, and the pictures and symbols of your creativity. Wake up to yourself and God. Now is the time to wake up.

After a lecture I gave on meditation, to a group of engineers from around the world, one man came up to validate meditation. He told me his life had been a disaster until he started meditating. He was unhappy and unable to get along with his wife, children or co-workers. After meditating for thirty minutes a day for several months, he was like a different person. He began to enjoy his family and work and was even happy with himself. He stated that meditation had brought him back to life.

You can manipulate your energies to create whatever you want. You can change your life by acknowledging your spirituality and allowing your spiritual self to take over. When you create as spirit, life takes on new meaning. Your conscious control of cosmic energies puts you back in charge of your creativity and your life.

Turn within to discover the glorious Cosmos waiting to awaken within you. Turn on your light of spirit and you can see the mysteries of the Cosmos clearly displayed within yourself. Meditate, use the spiritual techniques, make a commitment to yourself and your awakening will come easily. You will eventually awaken, even if you do not consciously move toward an aware state. Your awakening may not be as easy or pleasant, if you do not actively seek it or welcome it when it comes.

Let yourself take conscious control of your part in the Cosmic Play. You can manipulate the cosmic energies to exercise your creative power and learn your lessons. You have the power to desire and the faith to create. Do not be afraid to see and know who you are and what you are here to create. You can use meditation to discover your unique vibration and your place in the Cosmic Plan. Once you know your energy and what you are meant to do with it, you can consciously control your life to fulfill your purpose.

We are all part of a Cosmic Whole. Each of us has a purpose and the ability to fulfill that purpose. We are surrounded with validation for our spiritual experience, if we will quiet the physical information and listen to the spiritual message.

Now is the time for us to awaken to the fact that we are spirit and a part of God. We need to remember that we can manipulate cosmic energy and be the creators of our reality. We will join the awake consciousness of the Cosmos when we awaken to our spiritual nature.

God is everything. We are a part of God.

About the Author

Mary Ellen Flora is a spiritual teacher and healer of 19 years experience. She is co-founder of the CDM Psychic Institute and the author of the Key series of books and tapes on meditation, healing, clairvoyance and chakras. Throughout her life, she has used her psychic abilities to see auras, to see and communicate with spirit and to heal. She has dedicated her life to teaching others that they are spirit and a part of God, and that they can learn basic spiritual techniques to assist in their own spiritual awakening.

Mary Ellen resides in the Pacific Northwest where she teaches, provides psychic readings, writes, travels to give workshops, trains teachers and administers staff. She is married to M. F. "Doc" Slusher, the founder of CDM Psychic Institute and author of I Believe.

If you wish to contact Mary Ellen, please write to:

CDM Publications
2402 Summit Ave
Everett, WA 98201